JUSTIFICATION
BY
FAITH ALONE

Justification by Faith Alone

Charles Hodge

John W. Robbins
Editor

The Trinity Foundation

©1995 John W. Robbins
Published by The Trinity Foundation
Post Office Box 1666
Hobbs, New Mexico 88240

ISBN: 0-940931-42-7

CONTENTS

Foreword ix

Introduction xiii

Part I

Chapter 1 The Meaning of Justification 1

Chapter 2 Christ's Satisfaction of the Law 12

Chapter 3 The Righteousness of Christ 27

Part II

Chapter 4 Confessional Statements of the Doctrine 36

    The Westminster Standards 36

    The Heidelberg Catechism 36

    The Second Helvetic Confession 37

    Jonathan Edwards 41

    Points Included in the Above Statements

        of the Doctrine 42

Chapter 5 Justification Is a Forensic Act 45

    Proof of the Doctrine Just Stated 47

    Justification the Opposite of Condemnation 48

    Arguments from Equivalent Forms of Expression 49

    Argument from the Statement of the Doctrine 50

    The Apostle's Argument in the Epistle to the Romans 51

    Argument from the Ground of Justification 52

Justification Not Mere Pardon 53
Argument from the Immutability of the Law 53
Argument from the Nature of Our Union with Christ 55
Arguments from the Effects Ascribed to Justification 56
Summary 63
Calvin's Doctrine 63

Chapter 6 Works Not the Ground of Justification 67
Roman Catholic Doctrine 68
Arminian Doctrine 70
Protestant Doctrine 71

**Chapter 7 The Righteousness of Christ the Ground of
Justification** 77
Meaning of the Terms 79
The Righteousness of Christ Is the Righteousness of God ... 80

Chapter 8 Imputation of Righteousness 81

Chapter 9 Proof of the Doctrine 91
The Apostle's Argument 92
The Parallel Between Adam and Christ 95
Other Passages Teaching the Same Doctrine 97
Argument from the General Teaching of the Bible 100

**Chapter 10 The Consequences of the Imputation of
Righteousness** 105

Chapter 11 The Relation of Faith to Justification 111
Roman Catholic Doctrine 112
Arminian Doctrine 114
Protestant Doctrine 118

**Chapter 12 Objections to the Protestant Doctrine
of Justification** 120
It is said to lead to licentiousness 120
It is "inconsistent with the grace of the Gospel" 123
"God cannot declare the unjust to be just" 125

Chapter 13 Departures from the Protestant Doctrine 127
    Arminian Doctrine 127
    Summary 140
    Comparisons of the Different Doctrines 141

Scripture Index 143
Index 147
The Crisis of Our Time 154
Intellectual Ammunition 162

FOREWORD

The Trinity Foundation is to be commended for placing once again in print–and within one volume–the chapter on justification from Charles Hodge's *The Way of Life: A Handbook of Christian Belief and Practice* (1841), written at the request of the American Sunday School Union that it might be used by "intelligent and educated young persons, either to arouse their attention, or to guide their steps in the WAY OF LIFE," and the chapter on justification excerpted from the third volume of his famous *Systematic Theology* (1872-73).

This Trinity Foundation publication is a timely one, given the recent publication of the programmatic statement, "Evangelicals and Catholics Together: The Christian Mission in the Third Millennium," which appeared in *First Things* (May 1994)–a statement composed by eight Protestants (led by Charles Colson) and seven Roman Catholics (led by Richard John Neuhaus) and endorsed by twelve other Protestants and thirteen other Roman Catholics. While its call for co-belligerence against the rampant moral degeneracy in our nation's political, legal, medical, educational, and cultural life and for cooperation against social injustice and economic poverty is appropriate enough (Section IV), the statement's marginalizing of many of the stark theological differences which exist between Protestant Christianity and Roman Catholicism is inexcusable when its authors affirm their agreement on the Apostles' Creed and on the proposition that "we are justified by grace through faith because of Christ" (Section I) and then on this "confessional" basis call for an end to proselytizing each other's communicants and for a missiological ecumenism which cooperates together in evangelism and spiritual nurture (Section V).*

The word "alone" after the word "faith" in the statement's proposition on justification is thundering by its absence. As written, the statement is a capitulation to Rome's unscriptural understanding of justification, for never in the debate between Rome and the first Protestant Reformers did anyone on either side deny that sinners must be justified by faith. The whole controversy in the sixteenth century in this doctrinal area turned on whether sinners were justified by faith *alone (sola fide)* or by faith *and* good works which earned merit before God. The Protestant Reformers, following Paul's teaching on justification in Romans and Galatians, affirmed the former and denied the latter; Rome denied the former and affirmed the latter. And the Protestant Reformers, again following Paul (compare his entire argument in Galatians), maintained that the path the sinner follows here leads either to Heaven or to Hell. The Protestant Reformers clearly saw—over against Rome's doctrine of salvation which was (and still is) essential to the maintenance of its priestcraft and thus its economic fortunes–(1) that

---

* I am disappointed that Dr. James I. Packer, one of the statement's Protestant endorsers, lends the prestige of his name and his leadership position among evangelicals to this ecumenical statement, even though he acknowledges (1) that Rome's claim to be the only institution that can without qualification be called the church of Christ is theologically and historically flawed; (2) that Rome's teaching on the Mass and on merit cuts across Paul's doctrine of justification in and through Christ by faith; (3) that all of Rome's forms of the Mary cult, its invoking of saints, its belief in purgatory, and its continuing disbursement of indulgences, to say the least, "damp down the full assurance to which, according to Scripture, justification should lead through the ministry of the Holy Spirit"; and (4) that Rome's claim of infallibility for all conciliar and some papal pronouncements and its insistence that Christians should take their beliefs from the church rather than from the Bible make self-correction virtually impossible (compare Packer's article, "Why I Signed It," *Christianity Today* [Dec. 12, 1994], pp. 34-37).

I say I am disappointed by Packer, but I am not surprised, since Packer's ecclesiology in the area of ecclesiastical separation from unbelief has been suspect for years. As a member priest within and an advocate of the Anglican prelacy, Packer has lived within that communion and cooperated with it even though it tolerates and receives as "seminal thinkers" those who the Bible clearly declares are theological apostates. His willingness to evangelize and nurture converts with Roman Catholics is simply a further extension of this lapse in his understanding of Biblcal separation from unbelief.

saving faith is to be directed to the doing and dying of *Christ alone* and not to the good works or inner experience of the believer; (2) that the Christian's righteousness before God is *in Heaven* at the right hand of God in Jesus Christ and *not on Earth* within the believer; (3) that the ground of our justification is the vicarious work of Christ *for* us and not the gracious work of the Spirit *in* us; and (4) that the faith-righteousness of justification is not personal but vicarious, not infused but imputed, not experiential but judicial, not psychological but legal, not our own but alien to us, and not earned but graciously given through faith in Jesus Christ, which faith is itself a gift of grace. Hodge's two treatises on justification provide the Biblical ground and argumentation for these great teachings and drive home once again for the benefit of our theologically illiterate generation the reason why Luther called this doctrine the mark of a standing or falling church.

Before I close, a word about Charles Hodge the man is in order for those readers who may know little or nothing about him. Hodge (1797-1878) was the most influential American Presbyterian theologian of the nineteenth century, teaching at Princeton Theological Seminary from 1822 almost to his death in 1878 and editing the *Biblical Repertory and Princeton Review* from its inception in 1825 until 1871. During his teaching career more than three thousand ministerial students sat at his feet, most of whom became ministers in the Presbyterian church. Many of his writings—among them his commentaries on Romans, 1 and 2 Corinthians, and Ephesians, and his *magnum opus,* his three-volume *Systematic Theology*—still stand on evangelical preachers' shelves and are regularly consulted by them. I commend this worthy old Presbyterian stalwart to the Trinity Foundation readership as a trustworthy teacher and guide.

Robert L. Reymond
Professor of Systematic Theology
Knox Theological Seminary
January 1995

INTRODUCTION

In his letter to the churches in Galatia, Paul emphasizes the idea of justification by faith alone. In this letter Paul does not follow his usual pattern in writing to the churches: He does not praise the Galatians first and then reprimand them for their errors in later chapters; his rebuke begins in chapter 1. Paul writes:

> I marvel that you are turning away so soon from him who called you in the grace of Christ to a different gospel–which is not another–but there are some who trouble you and want to pervert the Gospel of Christ. But even if we or an angel from Heaven preach any other gospel to you than what we have preached to you, let him be accursed. As we have said before, so now I say again, if anyone preaches any other gospel to you than what you have received, let him be accursed.

The Gospel of justification by faith alone is obviously very important, so important that anyone–including Paul himself and angels from Heaven–who teaches a different gospel is cursed.

Paul illustrates both the meaning and the importance of justification by faith alone in chapter 2 of Galatians:

> But when Peter had come to Antioch, I withstood him to his face, because he was to be blamed. For before certain men came from James, he would eat with the Gentiles, but when they came, he withdrew and separated himself, fearing those who were of the circumci-

sion. And the rest of the Jews also played the hypocrite with him, so that even Barnabas was carried away with their hypocrisy. But when I saw that they were not straightforward about the truth of the Gospel, I said to Peter before them all, "If you, being a Jew, live in the manner of Gentiles and not as the Jews, why do you compel Gentiles to live as Jews? We who are Jews by nature and not sinners of the Gentiles, knowing that a man is not justified by the works of the law but by faith in Jesus Christ–even we have believed in Christ Jesus that we might be justified by faith in Christ and not by the works of the law, for by the works of the law no flesh shall be justified. . . . I do not set aside the grace of God, for if righteousness comes through the law, then Christ died in vain.

The meaning–the heart of the Gospel–is justification by faith alone. It was the most important doctrine of the first century, and it was the most important doctrine of the Christian Reformation in the sixteenth century. Almost all so-called Protestant churches in America–as well as the Roman Catholic church–do not believe and even deny the doctrine at the end of the twentieth century.

The importance Paul placed on justification by faith alone may be seen in his actions against Peter. Consider Peter: Peter was both an apostle and a disciple. His name had been given to him by Christ himself. Peter was an older man than Paul. He had lived and traveled with Jesus for three years. Peter had preached at Pentecost, opening the kingdom of God to all. The Roman Catholic church–but not the Bible–claims that Peter was the first pope, and as such, infallible. Yet Paul withstood Peter to his face, rebuking him publicly for his errors.

Consider also Paul: He was an apostle as well, though not a disciple. Younger than Peter, he had been a Pharisee of the Pharisees while Peter was a disciple of Christ. By the grace of God,

Paul had become a Christian while on his way to Damascus to persecute Christians. As a Christian who understood that salvation could not come from the law, Paul understood clearly that the doctrine of which Christians must be most jealous–for it is the heart of the Gospel–is justification by faith alone.

Consider what provoked Paul's vehement reaction to Peter: Peter had not preached a sermon against justification by faith alone; there is no suggestion that Peter made any false statements. Peter had simply withdrawn from eating with Gentile Christians, out of fear of the Jews, because the Old Testament law forbade eating with Gentiles. His actions, and those of Barnabas and the rest of the Jews, suggested that they thought that justification was not by faith alone, but by observation of the law. For this error Paul–the same Paul who repeatedly tells Christians to "be at peace among yourselves"–rebukes the apostle Peter publicly and disrupts the peace of the church at Antioch. Paul breaks the peace and publicly, not privately, corrects Peter for his hypocrisy that seems to cast doubt on the truth of justification by faith alone.

It was this doctrine–justification by faith alone–believed and preached by the Christians of the first century that turned the world upside down. It was this doctrine–justification by faith alone–that ended the dark millennium of Roman Catholic religious superstition in Europe in the sixteenth century when God caused the Reformers to believe and preach it again. And it is the doctrine of justification by faith alone that will turn the world upside down again when God causes his people to believe and preach it once more.

Justification by faith alone is the heart of the Gospel, and the Gospel is the power of God for salvation. If the world is to be saved in any sense, temporal or eternal, it will not be saved through our keeping of the law, but only through belief of the Gospel of Jesus Christ. Before Christ–except for the land of Israel, which had the revelation of God–there was nothing but pagan darkness and superstition throughout the world. After Christ, the Gospel was suppressed by wicked ecclesiastical and political powers–by spiritual wickedness in high places–and the world was again plunged into spiritual darkness.

Since the brilliant light of the Christian Reformation enlightened the world five centuries ago, its brilliance has dimmed and the Gospel has been suppressed, Christians have been persecuted by secular and religious powers, and Christian doctrines perverted. If God wishes his light and his truth to shine forth again in this present evil age, it will shine first and most brilliantly in a recovery of the doctrine of justification by faith alone.

John W. Robbins
December 1994

PART I

1
THE MEANING OF JUSTIFICATION

How can a man be just with God? The answer given to this question decides the character of our religion, and, if practically adopted, our future destiny. To give a wrong answer is to mistake the way to Heaven. It is to err where error is fatal, because it cannot be corrected. If God requires one thing, and we present another, how can we be saved? If he has revealed a method in which he can be just and yet justify the sinner, and if we reject that method and insist upon pursuing a different way, how can we hope to be accepted? The answer, therefore, which is given to the above question should be seriously pondered by all who assume the office of religious teachers and by all who rely upon their instructions. As we are not to be judged by proxy, but every man must answer for himself, so every man should be satisfied for himself what the Bible teaches on this subject. All that religious teachers can do is to endeavor to aid the investigations of those who are anxious to learn the way of life. And in doing this, the safest method is to adhere strictly to the instructions of the Scriptures and to exhibit the subject as it is there presented. The substance and the form of this all-important doctrine are so intimately connected that those who attempt to separate them can hardly fail to err. What one discards as belonging merely to the form, another considers as belonging to its substance. All certainty and security are lost as soon as this method is adopted, and it becomes a matter to be decided exclusively by our own views of right and wrong what is to be retained and what rejected from the Scriptural representations. Our only security, therefore, is to take the language of the Bible in its obvious meaning and put upon it the construction which the persons to whom it was addressed must have given, and which, consequently, the sacred writers intended it should bear.

As the doctrine of justification is not only frequently stated in the sacred Scriptures but formally taught and vindicated, all that will be attempted in this chapter is to give as faithfully as possible a representation of what the inspired writers inculcate on this subject; that is, to state what positions they assume, by what arguments they sustain those positions, how they answer the objections to their doctrine, and what application they make of it to the hearts and consciences of their readers.

It is one of the primary doctrines of the Bible, everywhere either asserted or assumed, that we are under the law of God. This is true of all classes of men, whether they enjoy a divine revelation or not. Everything which God has revealed as a rule of duty enters into the constitution of the law which binds those to whom that revelation is given and by which they are to be ultimately judged. Those who have not received any external revelation of the divine will are a law unto themselves. The knowledge of right and wrong, written upon their hearts, is of the nature of a divine law, having its authority and sanction, and by it the heathen are to be judged in the last day.

God has seen fit to annex the promise of life to obedience to his law. "The man who does those things shall live by them" (Romans 10:5) is the language of Scripture on this subject. To the lawyer who admitted that the law required love to God and man, our Savior said, "You have answered right: This do, and you shall live" (Luke 10:28). And to one who asked him, "What good things shall I do, that I may have eternal life?" he said, "If you will enter into life, keep the commandments" (Matthew 19:17). On the other hand, the law denounces death as the penalty of transgression: "The wages of sin is death" (Romans 6:23). Such is the uniform declaration of Scripture on this subject.

The obedience which the law demands is called righteousness, and those who render that obedience are called righteous. To ascribe righteousness to anyone, or to pronounce him righteous, is the Scriptural meaning of the word "to justify." The word never means to make good in a moral sense, but always to pronounce just or righteous. Thus God says, "I will not justify the wicked" (Exodus 23:7). Judges are commanded to justify the righteous and to condemn the wicked (Deuteronomy 25:1). Woe is pronounced on those who "justify the wicked for reward" (Isaiah 5:23). In the New Testament it is said, "By the deeds of the law there shall no flesh be justified in his sight" (Romans 3:20). "It is God that justifies. Who is he that condemns?" (Romans 8:33, 34). There is scarcely a word in the Bible the meaning of which is less open to doubt. There is no passage in the New Testament in which it is used out of its ordinary and obvious sense.* When God justifies a man he declares him to be righteous. To justify never means to render one holy. It is said to be sinful to justify the wicked, but it could never be sinful to render the wicked holy. And as the law demands righteousness, to impute or ascribe righteousness to anyone, is, in Scriptural language, to justify. To make (or constitute) righteous is another equivalent form of expression. Hence, to be righteous before God and to be justified mean the same thing as in the following passage: "Not the hearers of the law are just before God, but the doers of the law shall be justified" (Romans 2:13).

The attentive and especially the anxious reader of the Bible cannot fail to observe that these various expressions–to be righteous in the sight of God, to impute righteousness, to constitute righteous, to justify , and others of similar import–are so interchanged as to explain each other and to make it clear that to justify a man is to ascribe or impute to him righteousness. The great question then is, How is this righteousness to be obtained? We have reason to be thankful that the answer which the Bible gives to this question is so perfectly plain.

* Revelation 22:11 is probably no exception to this remark, as the text in that passage is uncertain.

In the first place, that the righteousness by which we are to be justified before God is not of works is not only asserted, but proved. The apostle's first argument on this point is derived from the consideration that the law demands a perfect righteousness. If the law were satisfied by an imperfect obedience, or by a routine of external duties, or by any service which men are competent to render, then indeed justification would be by works. But since it demands perfect obedience, justification by works is, for sinners, absolutely impossible. It is thus the apostle reasons, "As many as are of the works of the law are under the curse: For it is written, Cursed is every one that continues not in all things which are written in the book of the law to do them" (Galatians 3:10). As the law pronounces its curse upon every man who continues not to do all that it commands, and as no man can pretend to this perfect obedience, it follows that all who look to the law for justification must be condemned. To the same effect, in a following verse, he says, "The law is not of faith: but, the man that does them shall live in them." That is, the law is not satisfied by any single grace or imperfect obedience. It knows and can know no other ground of justification than complete compliance with its demands. Hence, in the same chapter Paul says, "If there had been a law given which could have given life, truly righteousness should have been by the law." Could the law pronounce righteous, and thus give a title to the promised life to those who had broken its commands, there would have been no necessity of any other provision for the salvation of men; but as the law cannot thus lower its demands, justification by the law is impossible. The same truth is taught in a different form when it is said, "If righteousness *come* by the law, then Christ is dead in vain" (Galatians 2:21). There would have been no necessity for the death of Christ if it had been possible to satisfy the law by the imperfect obedience which we can render. Paul therefore warns all those who look to works for justification that they are debtors to do the whole law (Galatians 5:3). It knows no compromise; it cannot demand less than what is right, and perfect obedience is right. Therefore its only language is as before, "Cursed is every one that continues not in all things which are written in the book of the law to do them" (Galatians 3:10); and, "The man which does those things shall live by them" (Romans 10:5). Every man, therefore, who expects justification by works must see to it, not that he is better than other men, or that he is very exact and does many things, or that he fasts twice in the week and gives tithes of all he possesses, but that he is *sinless*.

That the law of God is thus strict in its demands is a truth which lies at the foundation of all Paul's reasoning in reference to the method of justification. He proves that the Gentiles have sinned against the law written on their hearts, and that the Jews have broken the law revealed in their Scriptures; both Jews and Gentiles, therefore, are under sin, and the whole world is guilty before God. Hence, he infers, by the deeds of the law there shall no flesh be justified in his sight. There is, however, no force in this reasoning, except on the assumption that the law demands perfect obedience. How many men, who freely acknowledge that they are sinners, depend upon their works for acceptance with God! They see no inconsistency between the acknowledgment of sin and the expectation of justification by works. The reason is that they proceed upon a very different principle from that adopted by the apostle. They suppose that the law may be satisfied by very imperfect obedience. Paul assumes that God demands perfect conformity to his will, that his wrath is revealed against all ungodliness and unrighteousness of men. With him, therefore, it is enough that men have sinned to prove that they cannot be justified by works. It is not a question of degrees, more or less, for as to this point there is no difference, since "all have sinned, and come short of the glory of God" (Romans 3:23).

This doctrine, though so plainly taught in Scripture, men are disposed to think very severe. They imagine that their good deeds will be compared with their evil deeds, and that they will be rewarded or punished as the one or the other preponderates; or that the sins of one part of life may be atoned for by the good works of another; or that they can escape by mere confession and repentance. They could not entertain such expectations if they believed themselves to be under a law. No human law is administered as men seem to hope the law of God will be. He who steals or murders, though it be but once, though he confesses and repents, though he does any number of acts of charity, is not less a thief or murderer. The law cannot take cognizance of his repentance and reformation. If he steals or murders, the law condemns him. Justification by the law is for him impossible. The law of God extends to the most secret exercises of the heart. It condemns whatever is in its nature evil. If a man violate this perfect rule of right, there is an end of justification by the law; he has failed to comply with its conditions, and the law can only condemn him. To justify him would be to say that he had not transgressed.

Men, however, think that they are not to be dealt with on the principles of strict law. Here is their fatal mistake. It is here that they are in most direct conflict with the Scriptures, which proceed upon the uniform assumption of our subjection to the law. Under the government of God, strict law is nothing but perfect excellence; it is the steady exercise of moral rectitude. Even conscience, when duly enlightened and roused, is as strict as the law of God. It refuses to be appeased by repentance, reformation, or penance. It enforces every command and every denunciation of our Supreme Ruler, and teaches—as plainly as do the Scriptures themselves—that justification by an imperfect obedience is impossible. As conscience, however, is fallible, no reliance on this subject is placed on her testimony. The appeal is to the word of God, which clearly teaches that it is impossible a sinner can be justified by works, because the law demands perfect obedience.

The apostle's second argument to show that justification is not by works is the testimony of the Scriptures of the Old Testament. This testimony is urged in various forms. In the first place, as the apostle proceeds upon the principle that the law demands perfect obedience, all those passages which assert the universal sinfulness of men are so many declarations that they cannot be justified by works. He therefore quotes such passages as the following: "There is none righteous, no, not one; there is none that understands, there is none that seeks after God. They are all gone out of the way; they are together become unprofitable; there is none that does good, no, not one" (Romans 3:10-12). The Old Testament, by teaching that all men are sinners, does, in the apostle's view, thereby teach that they can never be accepted before God on the ground of their own righteousness. To say that a man is a sinner is to say that the law condemns him—and of course it cannot justify him. As the ancient Scriptures are full of declarations of the sinfulness of men, so they are full of proof that justification is not by works.

But in the second place, Paul cites their direct affirmative testimony in support of his doctrine. In the Psalms it is said, "Enter not into judgment with your servants, for in your sight shall no man living be justified" (Psalm 143:2). This passage he often quotes, and to the same class belong all those passages which speak of the insufficiency or worthlessness of human righteousness in the sight of God.

In the third place, the apostle refers to those passages which imply the doctrine for which he contends; that is, to those which speak of the acceptance of men with God as a matter of grace, as something which they do not deserve, and for which they can urge no claim founded upon their own merit. It is with this view that he refers to the language of David: "Blessed are they whose iniquities are forgiven and whose sins are covered. Blessed is the man to whom the Lord will not impute sin" (Romans 4:7, 8). The fact that a man is forgiven implies that he is guilty, and the fact that he is guilty implies that his justification cannot rest upon his own character or conduct. It need hardly be remarked, that, in this view, the whole Scriptures, from the beginning to the end, are crowded with condemnations of the doctrine of justification by works. Every penitent confession, every appeal to God's mercy is a renunciation of all personal merit, a declaration that the penitent's hope was not founded on anything in himself. Such confessions and appeals are indeed often made by those who still rely upon their good works or inherent righteousness for acceptance with God. This, however, does not invalidate the apostle's argument. It only shows that such persons have a different view of what is necessary for justification from that entertained by the apostle. They suppose that the demands of the law are so low that although they are sinners and need to be forgiven, they can still do what the law demands. Paul proceeds on the assumption that the law requires perfect obedience, and therefore every confession of sin or appeal for mercy involves a renunciation of justification by the law.

Again, the apostle represents the Old Testament Scriptures as teaching that justification is not by works by showing that they inculcate a different method of obtaining acceptance with God. This they do by the doctrine which they teach concerning the Messiah as a Redeemer from sin. Hence, Paul says that the method of justification without works (not founded upon works) was testified by the law and the prophets; that is, by the whole of the Old Testament. The two methods of acceptance with God—the one by works, the other by a propitiation for sin—are incompatible. And as the ancient Scriptures teach the latter method, they repudiate the former. They, moreover, in express terms assert that "the just shall live by faith." The law knows nothing of faith; its language is, "The man that does them shall live in them" (Galatians 3:11, 12). The law knows nothing of anything but obedience as the ground of acceptance. If the Scriptures say we are accepted through faith, they thereby say that we are not accepted on the ground of obedience.

Again: The examples of justification given in the Old Testament show that it was not by works. The apostle appeals particularly to the case of Abraham and asks whether he attained justification by works. He answers, No, for if he were justified by works he had whereof to glory; but he had no ground of glorying before God, and therefore he was not justified by works. And the Scriptures expressly assert, "Abraham believed God, and it was counted unto him for righteousness" (Romans 4:3). His acceptance, therefore, was by faith, and not by works.

In all these various ways does the apostle make the authority of the Old Testament sustain his doctrine that justification is not by works. This authority is as decisive for us as it was for the ancient Jewish Christians. We also believe the Old Testament to be the word of God, and its truths come to us explained and enforced by Christ and his apostles. We have the great advantage of an infallible interpretation of these early oracles of truth, and the argumentative manner in which their authority is cited and applied prevents all obscurity as to the real intentions of the sacred writers. That by the deeds of the law no flesh shall be justified before God is taught so clearly and so frequently in the New Testament, it is so often asserted, so formally proved, so variously assumed, that no one can doubt that such is indeed the doctrine of the Word of God. The only point on which the serious inquirer can even raise a question, is, What kind of works do the Scriptures mean to exclude as the foundation for acceptance with God? Does the apostle mean works in the widest sense, or does he merely intend ceremonial observances or works of mere formality, performed without any real love to God?

Those who attend to the nature of his assertions and to the course of his argument will find that there is no room for doubt on this subject. The primary principle on which his argument rests precludes all ground for mistaking his meaning. He assumes that the law demands perfect obedience, and as no man can render that obedience, he infers that no man can be justified by the law. He does not argue that because the law is spiritual it cannot be satisfied by mere ceremonies or by works flowing from an impure motive. He nowhere says that though we cannot be justified by external rites, or by works having the mere form of goodness, we are justified by our sincere, though imperfect, obedience.

On the contrary, he constantly teaches that since we are sinners, and since the law condemns all sin, it condemns us, and justification by the law is, therefore, impossible. This argument he applies to the Jews and the Gentiles without distinction–to the whole world, whether they knew anything of the Jewish Scriptures or not. It was the moral law, the law which he pronounced holy, just, and good, which says, "You shall not covet"; it is this law, however revealed–whether in the writings of Moses, or in the human heart–of which he constantly asserts that it cannot give life, or teach the way of acceptance with God.

As most of those to whom he wrote had enjoyed a divine revelation–and as that revelation included the law of Moses and all its rites–he of course included that law in his statement and often specially refers to it, but never in its limited sense (as a code of religious ceremonies) but always in its widest scope, as including the highest rule of moral duty made known to men. Hence he never contrasts one class of works with another, but constantly works and faith, excluding all classes of the former, works of righteousness as well as those of mere formality. "Not by works of righteousness which we have done, but according to his mercy he saved us" (Titus 3:5). "Who has saved us–not according to our works" (2 Timothy 1:9). We are saved by faith, not by works (Ephesians 2:9). Men are said to be justified without works, to be in themselves ungodly when justified; and it is not until they are justified that they perform any real good works. It is only when united to Christ that we bring forth fruit unto God. Hence, we are said to be "his workmanship, created in Christ Jesus unto good works" (Ephesians 2:10). All the inward excellence of the Christian and the fruits of the Spirit are the consequences–and not the causes–of his reconciliation and acceptance with God. They are the robe of beauty, the white garment, with which Christ arrays those who come to him poor, and blind, and naked. It is, then, the plain doctrine of the word of God that our justification is not founded upon our own obedience to the law. Nothing done by us or wrought in us can for a moment stand the test of a rule of righteousness which pronounces a curse upon all those who continue not in all things written in the book of the law to do them.

2

CHRIST'S SATISFACTION OF THE LAW

We have seen that the Scriptures teach, first, that all men are naturally under the law as prescribing the terms of their acceptance with God; and, second, that no obedience which sinners can render is sufficient to satisfy the demands of that law. It follows, then, that unless we are freed from the law, not as a rule of duty, but as prescribing the conditions of acceptance with God, justification is for us impossible. It is, therefore, the third great point of Scriptural doctrine on this subject that believers are free from the law in the sense just stated. "You are not under the law," says the apostle, "but under grace" (Romans 6:14). To illustrate this declaration, he refers to the case of a woman who is bound to her husband as long as he lives; but when he is dead, she is free from her obligation to him, and is at liberty to marry another man. So we are delivered from the law as a rule of justification and are at liberty to embrace a different method of obtaining acceptance with God (Romans 7:1-6). Paul says of himself that he had died to the law; that is, become free from it (Galatians 2:19). And the same is said of all believers (Romans 7:6).

He insists upon this freedom as essential not only to justification, but to sanctification. For while under the law, the motions of sins, which were by the law, brought forth fruit unto death; but now we are delivered from the law that we may serve God in newness of spirit (Romans 7:5, 6). Before faith came we were kept under the law, which he compares to a schoolmaster, but now we are no longer under a schoolmaster (Galatians 3:24, 25). He regards the desire to be subject to the law as the greatest infatuation. "Tell me," he says, "you that desire to be under the law, do you not hear the law?" and then shows that those who are under the demands of a legal system are in the condition of slaves and not of sons and heirs. "Stand fast therefore," he exhorts, "in the liberty wherewith Christ has made us free. Behold, I Paul say unto you, that if you be circumcised, Christ shall profit you nothing. For I testify again to every man that is circumcised that he is a debtor to do the whole law. Christ is become of no effect unto you, whosoever of you are justified by the law; you are fallen from grace (Galatians 4:21-31; 5:1-4).

This infatuation Paul considered madness, and exclaims, "O foolish Galatians, who has bewitched you that you should not obey the truth, before whose eyes Jesus Christ has been evidently set forth crucified among you? This only would I learn of you. Did you receive the Spirit by the works of the law or by the hearing of faith?" (Galatians 3:1-2). This apostasy was so fatal, the substitution of legal obedience for the work of Christ as the ground of justification was so destructive, that Paul pronounces accursed any man or angel who should preach such a doctrine for the Gospel of the grace of God.

It was to the law, as revealed in the books of Moses, that the fickle Galatians were disposed to look for justification. Their apostasy, however, consisted in going back to the law, no matter in what form revealed–to works, no matter of what kind, as the ground of justification. The apostle's arguments and denunciations, therefore, are so framed as to apply to the adoption of any form of legal obedience, instead of the work of Christ, as the ground of our confidence toward God. To suppose that all he says relates exclusively to a relapse into Judaism is to suppose that we Gentiles have no part in the redemption of Christ. If it was only from the bondage of the Jewish economy that he redeemed his people, then those who were never subject to that bondage have no interest in his work. And of course Paul was strangely infatuated in preaching

Christ crucified to the Gentiles. We find, however, that what he taught in the epistle to the Galatians, in special reference to the law of Moses, he teaches in the epistle to the Romans in reference to that law which is holy, just, and good, and which condemns the most secret sins of the heart.

The nature of the apostle's doctrine is, if possible, even more clear from the manner in which he vindicates it than from his direct assertions. "What then?" he asks, "shall we sin, because we are not under the law, but under grace? God forbid" (Romans 6:15). Had Paul taught that we are freed from the ceremonial, in order to be subject to the moral law, there could have been no room for such an objection. But if he taught that the moral law itself could not give life–that we must be freed from its demands as the condition of acceptance with God–then, indeed, to the wise of this world, it might seem that he was loosing the bands of moral obligation and opening the door to the greatest licentiousness. Hence the frequency and earnestness with which he repels the objection and shows that, so far from legal bondage being necessary to holiness, it must cease before holiness can exist; that it is not until the curse of the law is removed and the soul reconciled to God that holy affections rise in the heart and the fruits of holiness appear in the life. "Do we then make void the law through faith? God forbid: We establish the law" (Romans 3:31).

It is then clearly the doctrine of the Bible that believers are freed from the law as prescribing the conditions of their acceptance with God; it is no longer incumbent upon them, in order to justification, to fulfill its demand of perfect obedience, or to satisfy its penal exactions. But how is this deliverance effected? How is it that rational and accountable beings are exempted from the obligations of that holy and just law, which was originally imposed upon their race as the rule of justification? The answer to this question includes the fourth great truth respecting the way of salvation taught in the Scriptures. It is not by the abrogation of the law, either as to its precepts or penalty; it is not by lowering its demands, and accommodating them to the altered capacities or inclinations of men. We have seen how constantly the apostle teaches that the law still demands perfect obedience, and that they are debtors to do the whole law who seek justification at its hands. He no less clearly teaches that death is as much the wages of sin in our case as it was in that of Adam. If it is neither by abrogation nor relaxation that we are freed from the demands of the law, how has this deliverance been effected? By the mystery of vicarious obedience and suffering. This is the Gospel of the grace of God. This is what was a scandal to the Jews and foolishness to the Greeks; but to those that are called, the power of God and the wisdom of God (1 Corinthians 1:23, 24).

The Scriptures teach us that the Son of God–the brightness of the Father's glory and the express image of his person, who thought it not robbery to be equal with God–became flesh and subjected himself to the very law to which we were bound; that he perfectly obeyed that law and suffered its penalty, and thus, by satisfying its demands, delivered us from its bondage and introduced us into the glorious liberty of the sons of God. It is thus that the doctrine of redemption is presented in the Scriptures. "God," says the apostle, "sent forth his Son, made of a woman, made under the law, to redeem those that were under the law" (Galatians 4:4, 5). Being made under the law, we know that he obeyed it perfectly, brought in everlasting righteousness, and is therefore declared to be "the Lord our righteousness" (Jeremiah 23:6), since, by his obedience, many are constituted righteous (Romans 5:19). He, therefore, is said to be made righteousness unto us (1 Corinthians 1:30). And those who are in him are said to be righteous before God, not having their own righteousness, but that which is through the faith of Christ (Philippians 3:9).

That we are redeemed from the curse of the law by Christ's enduring that curse in our place is taught in every variety of form from the beginning to the end of the Bible. There was the more need that this point should be clearly and variously presented, because it is the one on which an enlightened conscience immediately fastens. The desert of death begets the fear of death. And this fear of death cannot be allayed until it is seen how, in consistency with divine justice, we are freed from the righteous penalty of the law. How this is done, the Scriptures teach in the most explicit manner. "Christ has redeemed us from the curse of the law, being made a curse for us" (Galatians 3:13). Paul has just said, "As many as are of the works of the law are under the curse." But all men are naturally under the law, and therefore all are under the curse. How are we redeemed from it? By Christ's being made a curse for us. Such is the simple and sufficient answer to this most important of all questions.

The doctrine so plainly taught in Galatians 3:13–that Christ has redeemed us from the curse of the law by bearing it in our stead–is no less clearly presented in 2 Corinthians 5:21: "He has made him who knew no sin to be sin for us, that we might be made the righteousness of God in him." This is represented as the only ground on which men are authorized to preach the Gospel. "We are ambassadors from Christ," says the apostle, "as though God did beseech you by us: We pray you in Christ's stead, be reconciled to God" (2 Corinthians 5:20). Then follows a statement of the ground upon which this offer of reconciliation is presented. God has made effectual provision for the pardon of sin by making Christ–though holy, harmless, and separate from sinners–sin for us, that we might be made righteous in him. The iniquities of us all were laid on him; he was treated as a sinner in our place in order that we might be treated as righteous in him.

The same great truth is taught in all those passages in which Christ is said to bear our sins. The expression, "to bear sin," is one which is clearly explained by its frequent occurrence in the sacred Scriptures. It means to bear the punishments due to sin. In Leviticus 20:17, it is said that he that marries his sister "shall bear his iniquity." Again, "Whoever curses his God shall bear his sin" (Leviticus 24:15). Of him that failed to keep the passover it was said, "That man shall bear his sin" (Numbers 9:13). If a man sin, he shall bear his iniquity.

It is used in the same sense when one man is spoken of as bearing the sin of another: "Your children shall wander in the wilderness forty years and bear your whoredoms" (Numbers 14:33). "Our fathers have sinned and are not; and we have borne their iniquities" (Lamentations 5:7). And when, in Ezekiel 18:20, it is said that "the son shall not bear the iniquity of the father," it is obviously meant that the son shall not be punished for the sins of the father. The meaning of this expression being thus definite, of course there can be no doubt as to the manner in which it is to be understood when used in reference to the Redeemer. The prophet says, "The Lord has laid on him the iniquity of us all. My righteous servant shall justify many, for he shall bear their iniquities. He was numbered with the transgressors, and he bore the sin of many" (Isaiah 53:6, 11, 12). Language more explicit could not be used. This whole chapter is designed to teach one great truth: that our sins were to be laid on the Messiah that we might be freed from the punishment which our sins deserved. It is therefore said, "He was wounded for our transgressions, he was bruised for our iniquities; the chastisement of our peace was upon him. For the transgression of my people was he stricken." In the New Testament, the same doctrine is taught in the same terms. "Who his own self bore our sins in his own body on the tree" (1 Peter 2:24). "Christ was once offered to bear the sins of many" (Hebrews 9:28). "You know that he was manifested to take away [to bear] our sins" (1 John 3:5). According to all these representations, Christ saves us from the punishment due to our sins by bearing the curse of the law in our stead.

Intimately associated with the passages just referred to are those which describe the Redeemer as a sacrifice or propitiation. The essential idea of a sin offering is propitiation by means of vicarious punishment. That this is the Scriptural idea of a sacrifice is plain from the laws of their institution, from the effects ascribed to them, and from the illustrative declarations of the sacred writers. The law prescribed that the offender should bring the victim to the altar, lay his hands upon its head, make confession of his crime; and that the animal should then be slain and its blood sprinkled upon the altar. Thus, it is said, "He shall put his hand upon the head of the burnt offering, and it shall be accepted from him to make atonement for him" (Leviticus 1:4). "And he brought the bullock for the sin offering; and Aaron and his sons laid their hands upon the head of the bullock for the sin offering" (Leviticus 8:14).

The import of this imposition of hands is clearly taught in the following passage: "And Aaron shall lay both his hands upon the head of the live goat and confess over him all the iniquities of the children of Israel and all their transgressions in all their sins, putting them upon the head of the goat. And the goat shall bear upon him all their iniquities unto a land not inhabited" (Leviticus 16:21, 22). The imposition of hands, therefore, was designed to express symbolically the ideas of substitution and transfer of the liability to punishment. In the case just referred to, in order to convey more clearly the idea of the removal of the liability to punishment, the goat on whose head the sins of the people were imposed was sent into the wilderness, but another goat was slain and consumed in its stead.

The nature of these offerings is further obvious from the effects attributed to them. They were commanded in order to make atonement, to propitiate, to make reconciliation, to secure the forgiveness of sins. And this effect they actually secured. In the case of every Jewish offender, some penalty connected with the theocratical constitution under which he lived was removed by the presentation and acceptance of the appointed sacrifice. This was all the effect, in the way of securing pardon, that the blood of bulls and of goats could produce. Their efficacy was confined to the purifying of the flesh and to securing, for those who offered them, the advantages of the external theocracy. Besides, however, this efficacy—which, by divine appointment, belonged to them considered in themselves—they were intended to prefigure and predict the true atoning sacrifice which was to be offered when the fulness of time should come. Nothing, however, can more clearly illustrate the Scriptural doctrine of sacrifices than the expressions employed by the sacred writers to convey the same idea as that intended by the term, "sin offering." Thus, all that Isaiah taught by saying of the Messiah that the chastisement of our peace was upon him; that with his stripes we are healed; that he was stricken for the transgression of the people; that on him was laid the iniquity of us all; and that he bore the sins of many, he taught by saying, "he made his soul an offering for sin." And in the epistle to the Hebrews it is said, he "was once offered [as a sacrifice] to bear the sins of many" (Hebrews 9:28). The same idea, therefore, is expressed by saying either he bore our sins or he was made an offering for sin. But to bear the sins of anyone means to bear the punishment of those sins; and, therefore, to be a sin offering conveys the same meaning.

Such being the idea of a sacrifice which pervades the whole Jewish Scriptures, it is obvious that the sacred writers could not teach more distinctly and intelligibly the manner in which Christ secures the pardon of sin than by saying he was made an offering for sin. With this mode of pardon all the early readers of the Scriptures were familiar. They had been accustomed to it from their earliest years. Not one of them could recall the time when the altar, the victim, and the blood were unknown to him. His first lessons in religion contained the ideas of confession of sin, substitution, and vicarious sufferings and death. When, therefore, the inspired penmen told men imbued with these ideas that Christ was a propitiation for sin, that he was offered as a sacrifice to make reconciliation, they told them, in the plainest of all terms, that he secures the pardon of our sins by suffering in our stead. Jews could understand such language in no other way; and, therefore, we may be sure it was intended to convey no other meaning. And, in point of fact, it has been so understood by the Christian church from its first organization to the present day.

If it were merely in the way of casual allusion that Christ

was declared to be a sacrifice, we should not be authorized to infer from it the method of redemption. But this is far from being the case. This doctrine is presented in the most didactic form. It is exhibited in every possible mode. It is asserted, illustrated, vindicated. It is made the central point of all divine institutions and instructions. It is urged as the foundation of hope, as the source of consolation, the motive to obedience. It is, in fact, *the Gospel.* It would be vain to attempt a reference to all the passages in which this great doctrine is taught. We are told that God set forth Jesus Christ as a propitiation for our sins through faith in his blood (Romans 3:25). Again, he is declared to be a "propitiation for our sins, and not for ours only: but also for the sins of the whole world" (1 John 2:2). He is called "the Lamb of God, which takes away [bears] the sin of the world" (John 1:29). "You were not redeemed," says the apostle Peter, "with corruptible things, as silver and gold, from your vain conversation received by tradition from your fathers; but with the precious blood of Christ, as of a lamb without blemish and without spot" (1 Peter 1:18, 19).

In the epistle to the Hebrews, this doctrine is more fully exhibited than in any other portion of Scripture. Christ is not only repeatedly called a sacrifice, but an elaborate comparison is made between the offering which he presented and the sacrifices which were offered under the old dispensation. "If the blood of bulls and of goats," says the apostle, "and the ashes of an heifer sprinkling the unclean sanctified to the purifying of the flesh, how much more shall the blood of Christ, who through the eternal Spirit [possessing an eternal spirit] offered himself without spot to God, purge your conscience from dead works to serve the living God?" (Hebrews 9:13, 14). The ancient sacrifices in themselves could only remove ceremonial uncleanness. They could not purge the conscience or reconcile the soul to God. They were mere shadows of the true sacrifice for sins. Hence, they were offered daily.

Christ's sacrifice, being really efficacious, was offered but once. It was because the ancient sacrifices were ineffectual that

Christ said, when he came into the world, "Sacrifice and offering you do not want, but a body you have prepared me: in burnt offerings and sacrifices for sin you have had no pleasure. Then said I, Lo, I come to do your will, O God." "By which will," adds the apostle, that is, by accomplishing the purpose of God, "we are sanctified [or atoned for] through the offering of the body of Jesus Christ once for all"; and by that "one offering he has perfected for ever them that are sanctified," and of all this, he adds, the Holy Ghost is witness (Hebrews 10:5-15).

The Scriptures, therefore, clearly teach that Jesus Christ delivers us from the punishment of our sins by offering himself as a sacrifice in our behalf. As under the old dispensation the penalties attached to the violations of the theocratical covenant were removed by the substitution and sacrifice of bulls and of goats, so under the spiritual theocracy, in the living temple of the living God, the punishment of sin is removed by the substitution and death of the Son of God. As no ancient Israelite, when by transgression he had forfeited his liberty of access to the earthly sanctuary, was ignorant of the mode of atonement and reconciliation; so now no conscience-stricken sinner, who knows that he is unworthy to draw near to God, need be ignorant of that new and living way which Christ has consecrated for us, through his flesh, so that we have boldness to enter into the holiest by the blood of Jesus.

In all the forms of expression hitherto mentioned–Christ was made a curse for us; he was made sin for us; he bore our sins; he was made a sin offering—there is the idea of substitution. Christ took our place, he suffered in our stead, he acted as our representative. But as the act of a substitute is in effect the act of the principal, all that Christ did and suffered in that character every believer is regarded as having done and suffered. The attentive and pious reader of the Bible will recognize this idea in some of the most common forms of Scriptural expression. Believers are those who are in Christ. This is their great distinction and most familiar designation. They are so united to him that what he did in their behalf they are declared to have done. When he died, they died; when he rose, they rose; as he lives, they shall live also. The passages in which believers are said to have died in Christ are very numerous. "If one died for all," says the apostle, "then all died" (not, "were all dead" as rendered in the King James Version) (2 Corinthians 5:14). He that died with Christ is justified from sin, that is, freed from its condemnation and power; and if we died with Christ, we believe that we shall live with him (Romans 6:7, 8). As a woman is freed by death from her husband, so believers are freed from the law by the body (the death) of Christ, because his death is in effect their death (Romans 7:3). And in the following verse, he says, having died (in Christ) we are freed from the law. Every believer, therefore, may say with Paul, I was crucified with Christ (Galatians 2:20).

In like manner, the resurrection of Christ secures both the spiritual life and future resurrection of all his people. If we have been united to him in his death, we shall be in his resurrection. If we died with him, we shall live with him (Romans 6:5, 8). "God," says the apostle, "has quickened us together with Christ; and has raised us up together and made us sit together in heavenly places in Christ Jesus" (Ephesians 2:4-6). That is, God has quickened, raised, and exalted us together with Christ.* It is on this ground, also, that Paul says that Christ rose as the firstfruits of the dead—not merely the first in order, but the earnest and security of the resurrection of his people. "For as in Adam all die, even so in Christ shall all be made alive" (1 Corinthians 15:20, 22). As our union with Adam secures our death, union with Christ secures our resurrection. Adam is a type of him who was to come—that is, Christ, inasmuch as the relation in which Adam stood to the whole race is analogous to that in which Christ stands to his own people. As Adam was our natural head, the poison of sin flows in all our veins. As Christ is our spiritual head, eternal life which is in him descends to all his members. It is not they who live, but Christ who

---

* There is no separate word in the original to answer to the word *together,* which is not to be understood of the union of believers with one another in the participation of these blessings. It is their union with Christ that the passage asserts.

lives in them (Galatians 2:20). This doctrine of the representative and vital union of Christ and believers pervades the New Testament. It is the source of the humility, the joy, the confidence which the sacred writers so often express. In themselves they were nothing and deserved nothing, but in him they possessed all things. Hence, they counted all things but loss that they might be found in him. Hence, they determined to know nothing, to preach nothing, to glory in nothing, but Christ and him crucified.

The great doctrine of the vicarious sufferings and death of Jesus Christ is further taught in those numerous passages which refer our salvation to his blood, his death, or his cross. Viewed in connection with the passages already mentioned, those now referred to not only teach the fact that the death of Christ secures the pardon of sin, but how it does it. To this class belong such declarations as the following: "The blood of Jesus Christ cleanses us from all sin" (1 John 1:7). "We have redemption through his blood" (Ephesians 1:7). He has "made peace through the blood of his cross" (Colossians 1:20). "Being now justified by his blood" (Romans 5:9). You "are made nigh by the blood of Christ" (Ephesians 2:13). "You are come to the blood of sprinkling" (Hebrews 12:22, 24). "Elect unto obedience and sprinkling of the blood of Jesus Christ" (1 Peter 1:2). "Unto him that loved us, and washed us from our sins in his own blood" (Revelation 1:5). "He has redeemed us unto God by his blood" (Revelation 5:9). "This cup," said the Son of God himself, "is the new testament in my blood, which is shed for many for the remission of sins" (Matthew 26:28, and Luke 22:20). The sacrificial character of the death of Christ is taught in all these passages. Blood was the means of atonement, and without the shedding of blood there was no remission; and, therefore, when our salvation is so often ascribed to the blood of the Savior, it is declared that he died as a propitiation for our sins.

The same remark may be made in reference to those passages which ascribe our redemption to the death, the cross, the flesh of Christ: These terms are interchanged as being of the same import. We are "reconciled to God by the death of his Son" (Romans 5:10). We are reconciled by his cross (Ephesians 2:16). We are "reconciled in the body of his flesh through death" (Colossians 1:21, 22). We are delivered from the law "by the body of Christ" (Romans 7:4); he abolished the law in his flesh (Ephesians 2:15); he took away the handwriting which was against us, nailing it to his cross (Colossians 2:14). The more general expressions respecting Christ's dying for us receive a definite meaning from their connection with the more specific passages above mentioned. Everyone, therefore, knows what is meant when it is said that "Christ died for the ungodly" (Romans 5:6); that he gave himself "a ransom for many" (Matthew 20:28); that he died "the just for the unjust, that he might bring us to God" (1 Peter 3:18). Not less plain is the meaning of the Holy Spirit when he said, God "spared not his own Son, but delivered him up for us all" (Romans 8:32); that he "was delivered for our offenses" (Romans 4:25); that he "gave himself for our sins" (Galatians 1:4).

Seeing, then, that we owe everything to the expiatory sufferings of the blessed Savior, we cease to wonder that the cross is rendered so prominent in the exhibition of the plan of salvation. We are not surprised at Paul's anxiety lest the cross of Christ should be made of no effect; or that he should call the preaching of the Gospel the preaching of the cross; or that he should preach Christ crucified, both to Jews and Greeks, as the wisdom of God and the power of God; or that he should determine to glory in nothing save the cross of Christ.

As there is no truth more necessary to be known, so there is none more variously or plainly taught than the method of escaping the wrath of God due to us for sin. Besides all the clear exhibitions of Christ as bearing our sins, as dying in our stead, as making his soul an offering for sin, as redeeming us by his blood, the Scriptures set him forth in the character of a priest, in order that we might more fully understand how it is that he effects our salvation. It was predicted, long before his advent, that the Messiah was to be a priest. "You are a priest forever after the order of Melchizedek," was the declaration of the Holy Spirit by the mouth of David (Psalm 110:4). Zechariah predicted that he should sit as "a priest upon his throne" (Zechariah 6:13). The apostle defines a priest to be a man "ordained for men in things pertaining to God, that he may offer both gifts and sacrifices for sins" (Hebrews 5:1).

Jesus Christ is the only real priest in the universe. All others were either pretenders or the shadow of the great high priest of our profession. For this office he had every necessary qualification. He was a man: "For inasmuch as the children were partakers of flesh and blood, he also took part of the same, in order that he might be a merciful and faithful high priest—one who can be touched with a sense of our infirmities, seeing he was tempted in all points like as we are, yet without sin." He was sinless: "For such an high priest became us, who was holy, harmless, and separate from sinners." He was the Son of God. The law made men, having infirmity, priests. But God declared his Son to be a priest who is consecrated forevermore (Hebrews 7:28).

The sense in which Christ is declared to be the Son of God is explained in the first chapter of the epistle to the Hebrews. It is there said that he is the express image of God; that he upholds all things by the word of his power; that all the angels are commanded to worship him; that his throne is an everlasting throne; that in the beginning he laid the foundations of the Earth; that he is from everlasting, and that his years fail not. It is from the dignity of his person, as possessing this divine nature, that the apostle deduces the efficacy of his sacrifice (Hebrews 9:14), the perpetuity of his priesthood (Hebrews 7:16), and his ability to save to the uttermost all who come unto God by him (Hebrews 7:25). He was duly constituted a priest. He glorified not himself to be made a high priest; but he that said unto him, "You are my Son," said also, "You are a priest forever."

He is the only real priest, and therefore his advent superseded all others, and put an immediate end to all their lawful ministrations by abolishing the typical dispensation with which they were connected. For the priesthood being changed, there was of necessity a change of the law. There was an annulling of the former commandment for the weakness and unprofitableness thereof, and there was the introduction of a better hope (Hebrews 7:12, 18, 19). He has an appropriate offering to present. As every high priest is appointed to offer sacrifices, it was necessary that this man should have something to offer. This sacrifice was not the blood of goats or of calves, but his own blood; it was himself he offered unto God to purge our conscience from dead works (Hebrews 9:12, 14). He has "put away sin by the sacrifice of himself," which was accomplished when he was "once offered to bear the sins of many" (Hebrews 9:26, 28). He has passed into the heavens. As the high priest was required to enter into the most holy place with the blood of atonement, so Christ has entered not into the holy places made with hands, "but into Heaven itself, now to appear in the presence of God for us" (Hebrews 9:24), and where "he ever lives to make intercession for us" (Hebrews 7:25).

Seeing then we have a great high priest that is passed into the heavens, Jesus the Son of God (let the reader remember what that means), who is set down on the right hand of the Majesty on high, having by himself purged our sins and made reconciliation for the sins of the people, every humble believer who commits his soul into the hands of this high priest may come with boldness to the throne of grace, assured that he shall find mercy and grace to help in time of need.

3

THE RIGHTEOUSNESS OF CHRIST

The Bible, as we have seen, teaches, first, that we are under a law which demands perfect obedience and which threatens death in case of transgression; second, that all men have failed in rendering that obedience, and therefore are subject to the threatened penalty; third, that Christ has redeemed us from the law by being made under it, and in our place satisfying its demands. It only remains to be shown that this perfect righteousness of Christ is presented as the ground of our justification before God.

In Scriptural language, condemnation is a sentence of death pronounced upon sin; justification is a sentence of life pronounced upon righteousness. As this righteousness is not our own, as we are sinners—ungodly, without works—it must be the righteousness of another, even of him who is our righteousness. Hence we find so constantly the distinction between our own righteousness and that which God gives. The Jews, the apostle says, being ignorant of God's righteousness and going about to establish their own righteousness, would not submit themselves unto the righteousness of God (Romans 10:3). This was the rock on which they shattered. They knew that justification required a righteousness; they insisted on urging their own, imperfect as it was, and would not accept that which God had provided in the merits of his Son, who is the end of the law for righteousness to everyone that believes.

The same idea is presented in Romans 9:30-32, where Paul sums up the case of the rejection of the Jews and the acceptance of believers. The Gentiles have attained righteousness, even the righteousness which is of faith. But Israel has not attained it. Why? Because they sought it not by faith, but as it were by the works of the law. The Jews would not receive and confide in the righteousness which God had provided, but endeavored, by works, to prepare a righteousness of their own. This was the cause of their ruin.

In direct contrast to the course pursued by the majority of his kinsmen, we find Paul renouncing all dependence upon his own righteousness, and thankfully receiving that which God had provided. Though he had every advantage and every temptation to trust in himself that any man could have, for he was one of the favored people of God, circumcised on the eighth day and touching the righteousness which is in the law, blameless; yet all these things Paul counted but loss, that he might win Christ and be found in him, not having his own righteousness, which is of the law, but that which is through the faith of Christ, the righteousness which is of God by faith (Philippians 3:4-9). Here the two righteousnesses are brought distinctly into view. The one was his own, consisting in obedience to the law; this Paul rejects as inadequate and unworthy of acceptance. The other is of God, and received by faith; this Paul accepts and glories in as all-sufficient and as alone sufficient. This is the righteousness which the apostle says God imputes to those without works. Hence it is called a gift, a free gift, a gift by grace, and believers are described as those who receive this gift of righteousness (Romans 5:17). Hence we are never said to be justified by anything done by us or wrought in us, but by what Christ has done for us. We are justified through the redemption that is in him (Romans 3:24). We are justified by his blood (Romans 5:9). We are justified by his obedience (Romans 5:19). We are justified by him from all things (Acts 13:39). He is our righteousness (1 Corinthians 1:30). We are made the righteousness of God in him (2 Corinthians 5:21). We are justified in his name (1 Corinthians 6:11). There is no condemnation to those who are in him (Romans 8:1). Justification is, therefore, by faith in Christ, because faith is receiving and trusting to him as our Savior, as having done all that is required to secure our acceptance before God.

It is thus, then, the Scriptures answer the question, How can a man be just with God? When the soul is burdened with a sense of sin, when it sees how reasonable and holy is that law which demands perfect obedience and threatens death as the penalty of transgression, when it feels the absolute impossibility of ever satisying these just demands by its own obedience and sufferings, it is then that the revelation of Jesus Christ as our righteousness is felt to be the wisdom and power of God unto salvation. Destitute of all righteousness in ourselves, we have our righteousness in him. What we could not do, he has done for us. The righteousness, therefore–on the ground of which the sentence of justification is passed upon the believing sinner–is not his own, but that of Jesus Christ.

It is one of the strongest evidences of the divine origin of the Scriptures that they are suited to the nature and circumstances of man. If their doctrines were believed and their precepts obeyed, men would stand in their true relation to God and the different classes of men to each other. Parents and children, husbands and wives, rulers and subjects would be found in their proper sphere and would attain the highest possible degree of excellence and happiness. Truth is in order to holiness. And all truth is known to be truth by its tendency to promote holiness. As this test, when applied to the Scriptures generally, evidences their divine perfection, so when applied to the cardinal doctrine of justification by faith in Jesus Christ, it shows that doctrine to be worthy of all acceptation. On this ground it is commended by the sacred writers. They declare it to be in the highest degree honorable to God and beneficial to man. They assert that it is so arranged as to display the wisdom, justice, holiness, and love of God, while it secures the pardon, peace, and holiness of men. If it failed in either of these objects, if it were not suited to the divine character or to our nature and necessities, it could not answer the end for which it was designed.

It will be readily admitted that the glory of God in the exhibition or revelation of the divine perfections is the highest conceivable end of creation and redemption; and consequently that any doctrine which is suited to make such an exhibition is, on that account, worthy of being universally received and gloried in. Now, the inspired writers teach us that it is peculiarly in the plan of redemption that the divine perfections are revealed; that it was designed to show unto principalities and powers the manifold wisdom of God; that Christ was set forth as a propitiatory sacrifice to exhibit his righteousness or justice; and especially that in the ages to come he might show forth the exceeding riches of his grace in his kindness toward us in Christ Jesus. It is the love of God–the breadth, length, depth, and height of which pass knowledge–that is here most conspicuously displayed. Some men strangely imagine that the death of Christ procured for us the love of God, but it was the effect and not the cause of that love. Christ did not die that God might love us; he died because God loved us. "God commends his love toward us in that, while we were yet sinners, Christ died for us" (Romans 5:8). He "so loved the world, that he gave his only begotten Son, that whoever believes in him should not perish, but have everlasting life" (John 3:16). "In this was manifested the love of God toward us, because God sent his only begotten Son into the world that we might live through him. Herein is love, not that we loved God, but that he loved us and sent his Son to be the propitiation for our sins" (1 John 4:9, 10).

As this love of God is manifested toward the unworthy, it is called grace, and this it is which the Scriptures dwell upon with such peculiar frequency and earnestness. The mystery of redemption is that a Being of infinite holiness and justice should manifest such wonderful love to sinners. Hence the sacred writers so earnestly denounce everything that obscures this peculiar feature of the Gospel–everything which represents men as worthy, as meriting, or, in any way by their own goodness securing the exercise of this love of God. It is of grace, lest any man should boast. We are justified by grace; we are saved by grace; and if of grace, it is no more of works, otherwise grace is no more grace (Ephesians 2: 8, 9; Romans 11:6). The apostle teaches us not only that the plan of salvation had its origin in the unmerited kindness of God, and that our acceptance with him is in no way or degree founded in our own worthiness; but, moreover, that the actual administraton of the economy of mercy is so conducted as to magnify this attribute of the divine character. God chooses the foolish, the base, the weak–those who are nothing–in order that no flesh should glory in his presence. Christ is made everything to us, that those who glory should glory only in the Lord (1 Corinthians 1:27-31).

It cannot fail to occur to every reader that unless he sincerely rejoices in this feature of the plan of redemption, unless he is glad that the whole glory of his salvation belongs to God, his heart cannot be in accordance with the Gospel. If he believes that the ground of his acceptance is in himself, or even wishes that it were so, he is not prepared to join in those grateful songs of acknowledgment to him who has saved us and called us with an holy calling, not according to our works, but according to his own purpose and grace, which it is the delight of the redeemed to offer unto him that loved them and gave himself for them. It is most obvious that the sacred writers are abundant in the confession of their unworthiness in the sight of God. They acknowledged that they were unworthy absolutely, and unworthy comparatively. It was of grace that any man was saved, and it was of grace that they were saved rather than others. It is, therefore, all of grace, that God may be exalted and glorified in all them that believe.

The doctrine of the gratuitous justification of sinners by faith in Jesus Christ not only displays the infinite love of God, but it is declared to be peculiarly honorable to him, or peculiarly consistent with his attributes, because it is adapted to all men. "Is he the God of the Jews only? Is he not also of the Gentiles? Yes, of the Gentiles also: Seeing it is one God who shall justify the circumcision by faith and uncircumcision through faith" (Romans 3:29, 30). "For the same Lord over all is rich unto all that call upon him. For *whoever* shall call upon the name of the Lord shall be saved" (Romans 10:12, 13). This is no narrow, national, or sectarian doctrine. It is as broad as the Earth. Wherever men, the creatures of God, can be found, there the mercy of God in Christ Jesus may be preached. The apostle greatly exults in this feature of the plan of redemption as worthy of God and as making the Gospel the foundation of a religion for all nations and ages. In revealing a salvation sufficient for all and suited for all, it discloses God in his true character, as the God and Father of all.

The Scriptures, however, represent this great doctrine as not less suited to meet the necessities of man than it is to promote the glory of God. If it exalts God, it humbles man. If it renders it manifest that he is a Being of infinite holiness, justice, and love, it makes us feel that we are destitute of all merit, and more, are most ill-deserving; that we are without strength; that our salvation is an undeserved favor. As nothing is more true than the guilt and helplessness of men, no plan of redemption which does not recognize these facts could ever be in harmony with our inward experience, or command the full acquiescence of the penitent soul. The ascription of merit which we are conscious we do not deserve produces of itself severe distress; and if this false estimate of our deserts is the ground of the exhibition of special kindness toward us, it destroys the happiness such kindness would otherwise produce. To a soul, therefore, sensible of its pollution and guilt in the sight of God, the doctrine that it is saved on account of its own goodness, or because it is better than other men, is discordant and destructive of its peace. Nothing but an absolutely gratuitous salvation can suit a soul sensible of its ill desert. Nothing else suits its views of truth or its sense of right. The opposite doctrine involves a falsehood and a moral impropriety in which neither the reason nor conscience can acquiesce.

The Scriptural doctrine, which assumes what we know to be

true–namely, our guilt and helplessness–places us in our proper relation to God–that relation which accords with the truth, with our sense of right, with our inward experience, and with every proper desire of our hearts. This is one of the reasons why the Scriptures represent peace as the consequence of justification by faith. There can be no peace while the soul is not in harmony with God, and there can be no such harmony until it willingly occupies its true position in relation to God. So long as it does not acknowledge its true character, so long as it acts on the assumption of its ability to merit or to earn the divine favor, it is in a false position. Its feelings toward God are wrong, and there is no manifestation of approbation or favor on the part of God toward the soul. But when we take our true place and feel our ill desert and look upon pardoning mercy as a mere gratuity, we find access to God; and his love is shed abroad in our hearts, producing that peace which passes all understanding. The soul ceases from its legal strivings; it gives over the vain attempt to make itself worthy, or to work out a righteousness wherewith to appear before God. It is contented to be accepted as unworthy, and to receive as a gift a righteousness which can bear the scrutiny of God. Peace, therefore, is not the result of the assurance of mere pardon, but of pardon founded upon a righteousness which illustrates the character of God; which magnifies the law and makes it honorable; which satisfies the justice of God while it displays the infinite riches of divine tenderness and love. The soul can find no objection to such a method of forgiveness. It is not pained by the ascription of merit to itself which is felt to be undeserved. Its utter unworthiness is not only recognized but openly declared. Nor is it harassed by the anxious doubt whether God can, consistently with his justice, forgive sin. For justice is as clearly revealed in the cross of Christ as love. The whole soul, therefore–however enlightened, or however sensitive– acquiesces with humility and delight in a plan of mercy which thus honors God, and which, while it secures the salvation of the sinner, permits him to hide himself in the radiance which surrounds his Savior.

The apostles, moreover, urge on men the doctrine of justification by faith with peculiar earnestness, because it presents the only method of deliverance from sin. So long as men are under the condemnation of the law, and feel themselves bound by its demands of obedience as the condition and ground of their acceptance with God, they do and must feel that he is unreconciled, that his perfections are arrayed against them. Their whole object is to propitiate him by means which they know to be inadequate. Their spirit is servile, their religion a bondage, their God a hard Master. To men in such a state, true love, true obedience, and real peace are alike impossible. But when they are brought to see that God, through his infinite love, has set forth Jesus Christ as a propitiation for our sins, that he might be just and yet justify those that believe–that it is not by works of righteousness which we have done, but according to his mercy he saves us–they are emancipated from their former bondage and made the sons of God. God is no longer a hard Master, but a kind Father. Obedience is no longer a task to be done for a reward; it is the joyful expression of filial love. The whole relation of the soul to God is changed, and all our feelings and conduct change with it. Though we have no works to perform in order to justification, we have everything to do in order to manifest our gratitude and love. "Do we then make void the law through faith? God forbid: We establish the law" (Romans 3:31). There is no such thing as real, acceptable obedience until we are thus delivered from the bondage of the law as the rule of justification and are reconciled to God by the death of his Son. Till then we are slaves and enemies, and have the feelings of slaves. When we have accepted the terms of reconciliation, we are the sons of God, and have the feelings of sons.

It must not, however, be supposed that the filial obedience rendered by the children of God is the effect of the mere moral influence arising from a sense of his favor. Though, perhaps, the strongest influence which any external consideration can exert, it is far from being the source of the holiness which always follows faith. The very act by which we become interested in the redemption of Christ from the condemnation of the law makes us partakers of his Spirit. It is not mere pardon or any other isolated blessing that is offered to us in the Gospel, but complete redemption, deliverance from evil, and restoration to the love and life of God. Those, therefore, who believe, are not merely forgiven, but are so united to Christ that they derive from and through him the Holy Spirit. This is his great gift, bestowed upon all who come to him and confide in him. This is the reason why he says, "Without me you can do nothing. As the branch cannot bear fruit of itself, except it abide in the vine; no more can you, except you abide in me. I am the vine, you are the branches: He that abides in me, and I in him, the same brings forth much fruit" (John 15:4, 5).

The Gospel method of salvation, therefore, is worthy of all acceptation. It reveals the divine perfections in the clearest and most affecting light, and it is in every way suited to the character and necessities of men. It places us in our true position as undeserving sinners; and it secures pardon, peace of conscience, and holiness of life. It is the wisdom and the power of God unto salvation. It cannot be a matter of surprise that the Scriptures represent the rejection of this method of redemption as the prominent ground of the condemnation of those who perish under the sound of the Gospel. That the plan should be so clearly revealed and yet men should insist upon adopting some other, better suited to their inclinations, is the height of folly and disobedience. That the Son of God should come into the world, die the just for the unjust, and offer us eternal life, and yet we should reject his proffered mercy, proves such an insensibility to his excellence and love, such a love of sin, such a disregard to the approbation and enjoyment of God, that–could all other grounds of condemnation be removed–this alone would be sufficient. "He that believes not is condemned already, because he has not believed in the name of the only begotten Son of God" (John 3:18).

PART II

4

CONFESSIONAL STATEMENTS
OF THE DOCTRINE

The Westminster Standards

Justification is defined in the Westminster Catechism: "An act of God's free grace, wherein he pardons all our sins, and accepts us as righteous in his sight, only for the righteousness of Christ imputed to us, and received by faith alone."

The Heidelberg Catechism

The Heidelberg Catechism in answer to the question, "How do you become righteous before God," answers,

Sola fide in Jesum Christum, adeo ut licet mea me conscientia accuset, quod adversus omnia mandata Dei graviter peccaverim, nec ullum eorum servaverim, adhæc etiamnum ad omne malum propensus sim, nihilominus tamen (modo hæc beneficia vera animi fiducia amplectar), sine ullo meo merito, ex mera Dei misericordia, mihi perfecta satisfactio, justitia, et sanctitas Christi, imputetur ac donetur; perinde ac si nec ullum ipse peccatum admisissem, nec ulla mihi

labes inhæreret; imo vero quasi eam obedientiam, quam
pro me Christus præstitit, ipse perfecte præstitissem.*

And in answer to the question, Why does faith alone justify?
it says: "Non quod dignitate meæ fidei Deo placeam, sed quod
sola satisfactio, justitia ac sanctitas Christi, mea justitia sit coram
Deo. Ego vero eam non alia ratione, quam fide amplecti, et mihi
applicare queam."†

The Second Helvetic Confession

The Second Helvetic Confession, chapter 15, says,

> Justificare significat Apostolo in disputatione de
> justificatione, peccata remittere, a culpa et pœna
> absolvere, in gratiam recipere, et justum pronunciare.
> Etenim ad Romanos dicit apostolus, "Deus est, qui
> justificat, quis ille, qui condemnet?" opponuntur
> justificare et condemnare. . . . Etenim Christus peccata
> mundi in se recepit et sustulit, divinæque justitiæ
> satisfecit. Deus ergo propter solum Christum passum
> et resuscitatum, propitius est peccatis nostris, nec illa
> nobis imputat, imputat autem justitiam Christi pro
> nostra: ita ut jam simus non solum mundati a peccatis
> et purgati, vel sancti, sed etiam donati justitia Christi,
> adeoque absoluti a peccatis, morte vel condemnatione,

---

* "Only by faith in Jesus Christ. My conscience accuses me as far as it can, that I
have gravely sinned against all of God's orders, and I have not observed any of them,
that until now I have been inclined to every evil; but nevertheless (provided that I
embrace these true benefits of the Spirit with confidence), Christ's perfect satisfaction, righteousness, and sanctity is reckoned and given to me without any merit of
my own, out of God's pure mercy; just as if I had not committed any sin, and as if no
disgrace were clinging to me; indeed, just as if I myself had perfectly shown that
compliance, which Christ has manifested for me." (All English translations are provided by the editor.)

† "Not because I please God with the worth of my faith, but because only Christ's
satisfaction, righteousness, and sanctity are my justice in the presence of God. But I
am able to be near this justice by no other method than by embracing faith."

justi denique ac hæredes vitæ æternæ. Proprie ergo loquendo, Deus solus nos justificat, et duntaxat propter Christum justificat, non imputans nobis peccata, sed imputans ejus nobis justitiam.*

These are the most generally received and authoritative standards of the Reformed Churches, with which all other Reformed symbols agree.

The Lutheran confessions teach precisely the same doctrine on this subject.†

Unanimi consensu, docemus et confitemur ... quod homo peccator coram Deo justificetur, hoc est, absolvatur ab omnibus suis peccatis et a judicio justissimæ condemnationis, et adoptetur in numerum filiorum Dei atque hæres æternæ vitæ scribatur, sine ullis nostris meritis, aut dignitate, et absque ullis præcedentibus, præsentibus, aut sequentibus nostris operibus, ex mera gratia, tantummodo propter unicum meritum, perfectissimam obedientiam, passionem acerbissimam, mortem et resurrectionem Domini nostri, Jesu Christi, cujus obedientia nobis ad justitiam imputatur.**

---

* "To justify, to the Apostle in debate about justification, means to forgive sins, to absolve from blame and punishment, to accept into grace, and to declare righteous. For indeed, as the apostle says to the Romans, 'God is he who justifies; who is he who condemns?' Justification and condemnation are opposites. . . . For indeed, Christ accepted the sins of the world into himself and removed them, and he made amends to divine justice. Therefore, God is gracious to our sins only because of Christ's suffering and resurrection, and he does not impute these sins to us; moreover, he reckons Christ's righteousness for us: so that now we are not only cleansed of our sins and purified, or virtuous, but also granted the righteousness of Christ and even absolved from sins, death, or condemnation; in short, we are suitable and proper for eternal life. Therefore, strictly speaking, God alone justifies us, and he justifies only because of Christ, not ascribing our sins to us but giving us his righteousness" (See Niemeyer, *Collectio Confessionum*, Leipzig, 1840.)

† The main passages are *Augsburg Confession*, Part I, Article IV; the *Apology* for that Confession, Article III; and the *Form of Concord*, Article III.

** "Agreeing unanimously, we teach and we make known . . . that man the sinner is justified in the presence of God, that is, he is absolved from all his own sins and from

Again,

Credimus, docemus, et confitemur, hoc ipsum nostram esse coram Deo justitiam, quod Dominus nobis peccata remittit, ex mera gratia, absque ullo respectu præcedentium, præsentium, aut consequentium nostrorum operum, dignitatis, aut meriti. Ille enim donat atque imputat nobis justitiam obedientiæ Christi; propter eam justitiam a Deo in gratiam recipimur et justi reputamur.*

Justificari significat hic non ex impio justum effici, sed usu forensi justum pronuntiari.[†]

And "Justificare hoc loco [Romans 5:1] forensi consuetudine significat reum absolvere et pronuntiare justum, sed propter alienam justitiam, videlicet Christi, quæ aliena justitia communicatur nobis per fidem."**

So also: "Vocabulum justificationis in hoc negotio significat justum pronuntiare, a peccatis et æternis peccatorum suppliciis

---

the judgment of a very justified condemnation, and he is adopted into the number of God's sons and appointed to eternal life, without any of our own deserving or worth, and without any of our own labors, past, present, or future—out of pure grace, only and just because of one unique merit: the most perfect obedience, the bitterest suffering, the death and resurrection of our Lord Jesus Christ, whose obedience is imputed to us for righteousness" (*Form of Concord*, III, 9).

* "We believe, we teach, and we make known that this itself is our justice in the presence of God, because the Lord has remitted our sins for us out of pure grace, without any regard for our own past, present, or future labors, for our own merit, or for our own worth. For he has reckoned and given to us the righteousness of Christ's compliance; because of this righteousness, we are accepted in grace by God and we are considered perfect (*ibid., Epitome*, III, 4).

[†] "To be justified here means not that a perfect man is produced from a godless one, but that he is pronounced perfect by a judicial exercise."

** "Justification in this passage [Romans 5:1] by judicial custom means to absolve the defendant and pronounce him perfect, but because of someone else's righteousness, namely Christ's, which alien righteousness is communicated to us through faith" (*Apology for the Augsburg Confession*, Article III, 131, 184).

absolvere, propter justitiam Christi, quæ a Deo fidei imputatur."*

Hase[†] concisely states the Lutheran doctrine on this subject in these words: "Justificatio est actus forensis, quo Deus, sola gratia ductus, peccatori, propter Christi meritum fide apprehensum, justitiam Christi imputat, peccata remittit, eumque sibi reconciliat."**

The *Form of Concord* says,

> Hic articulus, de justitia fidei, præcipuus est (ut Apologia loquitur) in tota doctrina Christiana, sine quo conscientiæ perturbatæ nullam veram et firmam consolationem habere, aut divitias gratiæ Christi recte agnoscere possunt. Id D. Lutherus suo etiam testimonio confirmavit, cum inquit: Si unicus his articulus sincerus permanserit, etiam Christiana Ecclesia sincera, concors et sine omnibus sectis permanet: sin vero corrumpitur, impossibile est, ut uni errori aut fanatico spiritui recte obviam iri possit.[††]

The Lutheran theologians, therefore, speak of it as the "ἀκρόπολυσ totius Christianæ religionis, ac nexus, quo omnia corporis doctrinæ Christianæ membra continentur, quoque rupto solvuntur."[‡]

---

* "The term *justification* in this matter means to pronounce perfect, to absolve from sins and from the eternal punishments of sins, because of Christ's righteousness, which is imputed by God through faith" (*Form of Concord,* III, 17. See Hase, *Libri Symbolici,* 3d edition, Leipzig, 1836).

† *Hutterus Redivivus,* § 109, 6th edition, Leipzig, 1845, p. 274.

** "Justification is a judicial act, by which God, led by grace alone, imputes Christ's righteousness to the sinner because of Christ's merit, which is acquired by means of faith; he forgives sins, and reconciles the sinner with himself."

†† "This article, concerning the righteousness of faith, is extraordinary (as the *Apologia* says) in the entire Christian doctrine, without which troubled consciences can never have true and firm consolation or properly understand the riches of Christ's grace. Luther also confirmed this with his own testimony when he said: If this one unique point remains uncorrupt, the Christian church will also remain uncorrupt, harmonious, and without all possible divisions; but if it is weakened, it is impossible for one mistaken or frenzied spirit to be properly corrected" (III, 6).

‡ "ἀκρόπολυσ of the whole Christian religion, and the connection by which all the

Jonathan Edwards

This statement of the doctrine of justification has retained confessional authority in the Lutheran and Reformed churches to the present day. President Edwards, who is regarded as having initiated certain departures from some points of the Reformed faith, was firm in his adherence to this view of justification, which he held to be of vital importance. In his discourse on "Justification by Faith Alone," he thus defines justification:

> A person is said to be justified when he is approved of God as free from the guilt of sin and its deserved punishment; and as having that righteousness belonging to him that entitles to the reward of life. That we should take the word in such a sense and understand it as the judge's accepting a person as having both a negative and positive righteousness belonging to him, and looking on him therefore as not only quit or free from any obligation to punishment, but also as just and righteous, and so entitled to a positive reward, is not only most agreeable to the etymology and natural import of the word, which signifies to make righteous, or to pass one for righteous in judgment, but also manifestly agreeable to the force of the word as used in Scripture.

He then shows how it is, or why faith alone justifies. It is not on account of any virtue or goodness in faith, but as it unites us to Christ and involves the acceptance of him as our righteousness. Thus it is we are justified "by faith alone, without any manner of virtue or goodness of our own."

The ground of justification is the righteousness of Christ imputed to the believer. "By that righteousness being imputed to us," says Edwards,

> is meant no other than this, that that righteousness of

---

limbs of the body of Christian doctrine are held together, and by which they are exempt from breaking" (Quenstedt).

Christ is accepted for us and admitted instead of that perfect inherent righteousness that ought to be in ourselves: Christ's perfect obedience shall be reckoned to our account so that we shall have the benefit of it, as though we had performed it ourselves. And so we suppose that a title to eternal life is given us as the reward of this righteousness. . . . The opposers of this doctrine suppose that there is an absurdity in it: They say that to suppose that God imputes Christ's obedience to us is to suppose that God is mistaken and thinks that we performed that obedience that Christ performed. But why cannot that righteousness be reckoned to our account and be accepted for us without any such absurdity? Why is there any more absurdity in it than in a merchant's transferring debt or credit from one man's account to another when one man pays a price for another, so that it shall be accepted, as if that other had paid it? Why is there any more absurdity in supposing that Christ's obedience is imputed to us than that his satisfaction is imputed? If Christ has suffered the penalty of the law for us and in our stead, then it will follow that his suffering that penalty is imputed to us, *i.e.*, that it is accepted for us and in our stead, and is reckoned to our account as through we had suffered it. But why may not his obeying the law of God be as rationally reckoned to our account as his suffering the penalty of the law?*

Points Included in the Above Statements of the Doctrine

According to the above statements, justification is
1. An act, and not, as sanctification, a continued and progressive work.
2. It is an act of grace to the sinner. In himself he deserves condemnation when God justifies him.

---

* *Works of President Edwards,* New York, 1868, Vol. IV, pp. 66, 91, 92.

3. As to the nature of the act, it is, in the first place, not an efficient act, or an act of power. It does not produce any subjective change in the person justified. It does not effect a change of character, making those good who were bad, those holy who were unholy. That is done in regeneration and sanctification. In the second place, it is not a mere executive act, as when a sovereign pardons a criminal and thereby restores him to his civil rights or to his former status in the commonwealth. In the third place, it is a forensic or judicial act, the act of a judge, not of a sovereign. That is, in the case of the sinner, or, *in foro Dei*, it is an act of God not in his character of sovereign, but in his character of judge. It is a declarative act in which God pronounces the sinner just or righteous, that is, declares that the claims of justice, so far as the sinner is concerned, are satisfied, so that he cannot be justly condemned, but is in justice entitled to the reward promised or due to perfect righteousness.

4. The meritorious ground of justification is not faith; we are not justified on account of our faith, considered as a virtuous or holy act or state of mind. Nor are our works of any kind the ground of justification. Nothing done by us or wrought in us satisfies the demands of justice or can be the ground or reason of the declaration that justice as far as it concerns us is satisfied. The ground of justification is the righteousness of Christ, active and passive, *i.e.*, including his perfect obedience to the law as a covenant, and his enduring the penalty of the law in our stead and on our behalf.

5. The righteousness of Christ is in justification imputed to the believer. That is, it is set to his account, so that he is entitled to plead it at the bar of God as though it were personally and inherently his own.

6. Faith is the instrument of justification. That is, God imputes the righteousness of Christ to the sinner when he (through grace) receives and rests on Christ alone for his salvation.

That such is the doctrine of the Reformed and Lutheran

churches on this important doctrine, cannot be disputed. The statements of the standards of those churches are so numerous, explicit, and discriminating as to preclude all reasonable doubt on this subject. That such is the doctrine of the Word of God appears from the following consideration.

It will not be necessary to discuss all the points above specified separately, as some of them are necessarily included in others. The following propositions include all the essential points of the doctrine.

5

JUSTIFICATION IS A FORENSIC ACT

By this the Reformers intended, in the first place, to deny the Romish doctrine of subjective justification; that is, that justification consists in an act or agency of God making the sinner subjectively holy. Romanists confound or unite justification and sanctification. They define justification as "the remission of sin and infusion of new habits of grace." By remission of sin they mean not simply pardon, but the removal of everything of the nature of sin from the soul. Justification, therefore, with them, is purely subjective, consisting in the destruction of sin and the infusion of holiness. In opposition to this doctrine, the Reformers maintained that by *justification* the Scriptures mean something different from sanctification; that the two gifts, although inseparable, are distinct; and that justification, instead of being an efficient act changing the inward character of the sinner, is a declarative act announcing and determining his relation to the law and justice of God.

In the second place, the confessions of the Reformation no less explicitly teach that justification is not simply pardon and restoration. It includes pardon, but it also includes a declaration that the believer is just or righteous in the sight of the law. He has a right to plead a righteousness which completely satisfies its demands.

And, therefore, in the third place, affirmatively, those confessions teach that justification is a judicial or forensic act, *i.e.,* an act of God as judge proceeding according to law declaring that the sinner is just, *i.e.,* that the law no longer condemns him, but acquits and pronounces him to be entitled to eternal life.

Here, as so often in other cases, the ambiguity of words is apt to create embarassment. The Greek word δίκαιος and the English word *righteous* have two distinct senses. They sometimes express moral character. When we say that God is righteous, we mean that he is right. He is free from any moral imperfection. So when we say that a man is righteous, we generally mean that he is upright and honest; that he is and does what he ought to be and do. In this sense the word expresses the relation which a man sustains to the rule of moral conduct. At other times, however, these words express, not moral character, but the relation which a man sustains to justice. In this sense a man is just with regard to whom justice is satisfied or against whom justice has no demands. The lexicons, therefore, tell us that δίκαιος sometimes means *leges observans*; at others, *insons, culpa vacans* (free from guilt or obligation to punishment)–*judicio Dei insons*. Pilate (Matthew 27:24) said, "I am innocent of the blood of this just person"; *i.e.,* of this person who is free from guilt; free from anything which justifies his condemnation to death. "Christ, also," says the Apostle, "has once suffered for sins, the just for the unjust"; the innocent for the guilty (1 Peter 3:18). See Romans 2:13; 5:19. "As by one man's disobedience many were made sinners, so by the obedience of one shall many be made righteous."

As the predicate of *judicandus* in his relation to the judge, "righteousness" expresses, not a positive virtue, but a judicial negative freedom from *reatus*. In the presence of his judge, he is צַדִּיק who stands free from guilt and desert of punishment (*straflos*), either because he has contracted no guilt (as, *e.g.,* Christ), or, because in the way demanded by the Judge (under the Old Testament by expiatory sacrifice) he has expiated the guilt contracted.*

---

* *Christliche Dogmatik,* Johannes Heinrich August Ebrard. § 402 (Königsberg edition, 1852), Vol. II, p. 163.

If, therefore, we take the word *righteous* in the former of the two senses above mentioned, when it expresses moral character, it would be a contradiction to say that God pronounces the sinner righteous. This would be equivalent to saying that God pronounces the sinner to be not a sinner, the wicked to be good, the unholy to be holy. But if we take the word in the sense in which the Scriptures so often use it, as expressing relation to justice, then when God pronounces the sinner righteous or just, he simply declares that his guilt is expiated, that justice is satisfied, that he has the righteousness which justice demands. This is precisely what Paul says when he says that God "justifies the ungodly" (Romans 4:5). God does not pronounce the ungodly to be godly; he declares that notwithstanding the sinner's personal sinfulness and unworthiness, he is accepted as righteous on the ground of what Christ has done for him.

Proof of the Doctrine Just Stated

That *to justify* means neither simply *to pardon*, nor *to make inherently righteous* or *good* is proved by the uniform usage of the word *to justify* in Scripture. It is never used in either of those senses, but always *to declare* or *pronounce just*. It is unnecessary to cite passages in proof of a usage which is uniform. The few following examples are enough. Deuteronomy 25:1: "If there be a controversy between men, and they come into judgment, that the judges may judge them; then they shall justify the righteous, and condemn the wicked." Exodus 23:7: "I will not justify the wicked." Isaiah 5:23: "Which justify the wicked for reward." Proverbs 17:15: "He that justifies the wicked" is "abomination to the Lord." Luke 10:29: "He willing to justify himself." Luke 16:15: "You are they which justify yourselves before men." Matthew 11:19: "Wisdom is justifed by her children." Galatians 2:16: "A man is not justified by the works of the law." Galatians 5:4: "Whosoever of you are justified by the law; you are fallen from grace." Thus men are said to justify God. Job 32:2: "Because he justified himself, rather than God." Psalm 51:4: "That you might be justified when you speak." Luke 7:29: "All the people that heard him, and the publicans, justified God." The only passage in the New Testament where the word δικαιόω seems to be used in a different sense is Revelation 22:11: ὁ δίκαιος δικαιωθήτω ἔτι, "He that is righteous, let him be righteous still." Here the first aorist passive appears to be used in a middle sense: "Let him show himself righteous, or continue righteous." Even if the reading in this passage were undoubted, this single case would have no force against the established usage of the word. The reading, however, is not merely doubtful, but it is, in the judgment of the majority of the critical editors, Tischendorf among the rest, incorrect. They give, as the true text, δικαιοσύνην ποιησάτω ἔτι. Even if this latter reading be, as De Wette thinks, a gloss, it shows that ὁ δίκαιος δικαιωθήτω ἔτι was as intolerable to a Greek ear as the expression, "He that is righteous, let him justify himself still" would be to us.

The usage of common life as to this word is just as uniform as that of the Bible. It would be a perfect solecism to say of a criminal whom the executive had pardoned that he was justified; or that a reformed drunkard or thief was justified. The word always expresses a judgment, whether of the mind, as when one man justifies another for his conduct, or officially of a judge. If such be the established meaning of the word, it ought to settle all controversy as to the nature of justification. We are bound to take the words of Scripture in their true established sense. And, therefore, when the Bible says, "God justifies the believer," we are not at liberty to say that it means that he pardons, or that he sanctifies him. It means, and can mean only, that he pronounces him just.

Justification the Opposite of Condemnation

This is still further evident from the antithesis between condemnation and justification. Condemnation is not the opposite either of pardon or of reformation. To condemn is to pronounce guilty or worthy of punishment. To justify is to declare not guilty, or that justice does not demand punishment, or that the person concerned cannot justly be condemned. When, therefore, the Apostle says (Romans 8:1), "There is, therefore, now no condemantion to them which are in Christ Jesus," he declares that they are absolved from guilt; that the penalty of the law cannot justly be inflicted upon them. "Who," he asks, "shall lay anything to the charge of God's elect? God who justifies? Who is he that condemns? Christ who died?" (33, 34). Against the elect in Christ no ground of condemnation can be presented. God pronounces them just, and therefore no one can pronounce them guilty.

This passage is certainly decisive against the doctrine of subjective justification in any form. This opposition between condemnation and justification is familiar both in Scripture and in common life. Job 9:20: "If I justify myself, my own mouth shall condemn me." Job 34:17: "And will you condemn him that is most just?" If *to condemn* does not mean to make wicked, *to justify* does not mean to make good. And if condemnation is a judicial as opposed to an executive act, so is justification. In condemnation it is a judge who pronounces sentence on the guilty. In justification it is a judge who pronounces or who declares the person arraigned free from guilt and entitled to be treated as righteous.

Argument from Equivalent Forms of Expression

The forms of expression which are used as equivalents of the word *justify* clearly determine the nature of the act. Thus Paul speaks of "the blessedness of the man unto whom God imputes righteousness without works" (Romans 4:6). To impute righteousness is not to pardon; neither is it to sanctify. It means to justify, *i.e.*, to attribute righteousness. The negative form in which justification is described is equally significant. "Blessed are they whose iniquities are forgiven, and whose sins are covered. Blessed is the man to whom the Lord will not impute sin" (Romans 4:7-8). As *to impute sin* never means and cannot mean to make wicked; so the negative statement *not to impute sin* cannot mean to sanctify. And as *to impute sin* does mean to lay sin to one's account and to treat him accordingly; so *to justify* means to lay righteousness to one's account and treat him accordingly. "God sent not his Son into the world to condemn the world. . . . He that believes on him is not condemned; but he that believes not is condemned already" (John 3:17, 18).

For "as by the offense of one judgment came upon all men to condemnation; even so by the righteousness of one the free gift came upon all men unto justification of life" (Romans 5:18). It was κρῖμα, a judicial sentence, which came on men for the offense of Adam, and it is a judicial sentence (justification, a δικαίωσις) which comes for the righteousness of Christ; or, as is said in verse 16 of the same chapter, it was a κρῖμα εἰς κατάκριμα, a condemnatory sentence that came for one offense; and a χάρισμα εἰς δικαίωμα, a sentence of gratuitous justication from many offenses. Language cannot be plainer. If a sentence of condemnation is a judicial act, then justification is a judicial act.

Argument from the Statement of the Doctrine

The judicial character of justification is involved in the mode in which the doctrine is presented in the Bible. The Scriptures speak of law, of its demands, of its penalty, of sinners as arraigned at the bar of God, of the day of judgment. The question is, How shall man be just with God? The answer to this question determines the whole method of salvation. The question is not, How can a man become holy? but, How can he become just? How can he satisfy the claims which justice has against him?

It is obvious that if there is no such attribute as justice in God, if what we call justice is only benevolence, then there is no pertinency in this question. In that case, man is not required to be just in order to be saved. There would be no claims of justice to be satisfied. Repentance is all that would need to be rendered as the condition of restoration to the favor of God. Or, any didactic declaration or exhibition of God's disapprobation of sin would open the way for the safe pardon of sinners. Or, if the demands of justice were easily satisfied–if partial, imperfect obedience and fatherly chastisements, or self-inflicted penances, would suffice to satisfy its claims–then the sinner need not be just with God in order to be saved. But the human soul knows intuitively that these are refuges of lies. It knows that there is such an attribute as justice. It knows that the demands thereof are inexorable because they are righteous. It knows that it cannot be saved unless it be justified, and it knows that it cannot be declared just unless the demands of justice are fully satisfied. Low views of the evil of sin and of the justice of God lie at the foundation of all false views of this great doctrine.

The Apostle's Argument in the Epistle to the Romans

The Apostle begins the discussion of this subject by assuming that the justice of God, his purpose to punish all sin, to demand perfect conformity to his law, is revealed from Heaven, *i.e.*, so revealed that no man, whether Jew or Gentile, can deny it (Romans 1:18). Men, even the most degraded pagans, know the righteous judgment of God that those who sin are worthy of death (verse 32). He next proves that all men are sinners and, being sinners, are under condemnation. The whole world is "guilty before God" (Romans 3:19). From this he infers, as intuitively certain (because plainly included in the premises), that no flesh living can be justified before God "by the deeds of the law," *i.e.*, on the ground of his own character and conduct. If guilty he cannot be pronounced not guilty, or just. In Paul's argument, to justify is to pronounce just. Δίκαιοσ is the opposite of ὑπόδικοσ (*i.e.*, "reus, satisfactionem alteri debens"). That is, *righteous* is the opposite of *guilty.* To pronounce guilty is to condemn. To pronounce righteous, *i.e.,* not guilty, is to justify. If a man denies the authority of Scripture, or if he feels at liberty (while holding what he considers the substance of Scripture doctrines) to reject the form, it is conceivable that he may deny that justification is a judicial act; but it seems impossible that any one should deny that it is so represented in the Bible. Some men, professing to believe the Bible, deny that there is anything supernatural in the work of regeneration and sanctification. "Being born of the Spirit"; "quickened by the mighty power of God"; "created anew in Christ Jesus" are only, they say, strong oriental expressions for a self-wrought reformation. By a similar process it is easy to get rid, not only of the doctrine of justification as a judicial act, but of all other distinguishing doctrines of the Scriptures. This, however, is not to interpret, but to pervert.

The Apostle, having taught that God is just, *i.e.,* that he demands the satisfaction of justice, and that men are sinners and can render no such satisfaction themselves, announces that such a righteousness has been provided and is revealed in the Gospel. It is not our own righteousness, which is of the law, but the righteousness of Christ, and, therefore, the righteousness of God, in virtue of which and on the ground of which God can be just and yet justify the sinner who believes in Christ. As long as the Bible stands, this must stand as a simple statement of what Paul teaches as to the method of salvation. Men may dispute as to what he means, but this is surely what he says.

Argument from the Ground of Justification

The nature of justification is determined by its ground. This indeed is an anticipation of another part of the subject, but it is in point here. If the Bible teaches that the ground of justification–the reason why God remits to us the penalty of the law and accepts us as righteous in his sight–is something out of ourselves, something done for us and not what we do or experience, then it of necessity follows that justification is not subjective. It does not consist in the infusion of righteousness or in making the person justified personally holy. If the "formal cause" of our justification be our goodness, then we are justified for what we are. The Bible, however, teaches that no man living can be justified for what he is. He is condemned for what he is and for what he does. He is justified for what Christ has done for him.

Justification Not Mere Pardon

For the same reason, justification cannot be mere pardon. Pardon does not proceed on the ground of a satisfaction. A prisoner delivered by a ransom is not pardoned. A debtor whose obligations have been cancelled by a friend becomes entitled to freedom from the claims of his creditor. When a sovereign pardons a criminal, it is not an act of justice. It is not on the ground of satisfaction to the law. The Bible, therefore, in teaching that justification is on the ground of an atonement or satisfaction; that the sinner's guilt is expiated; that he is redeemed by the precious blood of Christ; and that judgment is pronounced upon him as righteous, does thereby teach that justification is neither pardon nor infusion of righteousness.

Argument from the Immutability of the Law

The doctrine that justification consists simply in pardon and consequent restoration assumes that the divine law is imperfect and mutable. In human governments it is often expedient and right that men justly condemned to suffer the penalty of the law should be pardoned. Human laws must be general. They cannot take in all the circumstances of each particular case. Their execution would often work hardship or injustice. Human judgments may therefore often be set aside. It is not so with the divine law. The law of the

Lord is perfect. And being perfect it cannot be disregarded. It demands nothing which ought not to be demanded. It threatens nothing which ought not to be inflicted. It is in fact its own executioner. Sin is death (Romans 8:6). The justice of God makes punishment as inseparable from sin as life is from holiness. The penalty of the law is immutable and as little capable of being set aside as the precept. Accordingly, the Scriptures everywhere teach that in the justification of the sinner there is no relaxation of the penalty. There is no setting aside or disregarding the demands of the law. We are delivered from the law, not by its abrogation, but by its execution (Galatians 2:19). We are freed from the law by the body of Christ (Romans 7:4). Christ, having taken our place, bore our sins in his own body on the tree (1 Peter 2:24). The handwriting which was against us, he took out of the way, nailing it to his cross (Colossians 2:14). We are therefore not under the law, but under grace (Romans 6:14). Such representations are inconsistent with the theory which supposes that the law may be dispensed with; that the restoration of sinners to the favor and fellowship of God requires no satisfaction to its demands; that the believer is pardoned and restored to fellowship with God, just as a thief or forger is pardoned and restored to his civil rights by the executive in human governments. This is against the Scriptures. God is just in justifying the sinner. He acts according to justice.

It will be seen that everything in this discussion turns on the question: Is there is such an attribute in God as justice? If justice be only "benevolence guided by wisdom," then there is no justification. What evangelical Christians so regard is only pardon or sanctification. But if God, as the Scriptures and conscience teach, be a just God–as immutable in his justice as in his goodness and truth–then there can be no remission of the penalty of sin except on the ground of expiation, and no justification except on the ground of the satisfaction of justice; and therefore justification must be a judicial act, and neither simply pardon nor the infusion of righteousness. These doctrines sustain each other. What the Bible teaches of the justice of God proves that justification is a judicial declaration that justice is satisfied. And what the Bible teaches of the nature of justification proves that justice in God is something more than benevolence. It is thus that all the great doctrines of the Bible are concatenated.

Argument from the Nature of Our Union with Christ

The theory which reduces justification to pardon and its consequences is inconsistent with what is revealed concerning our union with Christ. That union is mystical, supernatural, representative, and vital. We were in him before the foundation of the world (Ephesians 1:4); we are in him as we were in Adam (Romans 5:12, 21; 1 Corinthians 15:22); we are in him as the members of the body are in the head (Ephesians 1:23, 4:16; 1 Corinthians 12:12, 27); we are in him as the branches are in the vine (John 15:1-12). We are in him in such a sense that his death is our death, we were crucified with him (Galatians 2:20; Romans 6:1-8); we are so united with him that we rose with him and sit with him in heavenly places (Ephesians 2:1-6). In virtue of this union we are (in our measure) what he is. We are the sons of God in him. And what he did, we did. His righteousness is our righteousness. His life is our life. His exaltation is our exaltation. Such is the pervading representation of the Scriptures.

All this is overlooked by the advocates of the opposite theory. According to that view, Christ is no more united to his people (except in sentiment) than to other men. He has simply done what renders it consistent with the character of God and the interests of his kingdom to pardon any and every man who repents and believes. His relation is purely external. He is not so united to his people that his merit becomes their merit and his life their life. Christ is not in them the hope of glory (Colossians 1:27). He is not of God made unto them wisdom, righteousness, sanctification, and redemption (1 Corinthians 1:30). They are not so in him that, in virtue of that union, they are filled with all the fulness of God (Colossians 2:10; and Ephesians 3:19). On the other hand, the Protestant doctrine of justification harmonizes with all these representations. If we are so united to Christ as to be made partakers of his life, we are also partakers of his righteousness. What he did in obeying and suffering he did for his people. One essential element of his redeeming work was to satisfy the demands of justice in their behalf, so that in him and for his sake they are entitled to pardon and eternal life.

Arguments from the Effects Ascribed to Justification

The consequences attributed to justification are inconsistent with the assumption that it consists either in pardon or in the infusion of righteousness. Those consequences are peace, reconciliation, and a title to eternal life. "Being justified by faith," says the Apostle, "we have peace with God" (Romans 5:1). But pardon does not produce peace. It leaves the conscience unsatisfied. A pardoned criminal is not only just as much a criminal as he was before, but his sense of guilt and remorse of conscience are in no degree lessened. Pardon can remove only the outward and arbitrary penalty. The sting of sin remains. There can be no satisfaction to the mind until there is satisfaction of justice.

Justification secures peace, not merely because it includes pardon, but because that pardon is dispensed on the ground of a full satisfaction of justice. What satisfies the justice of God satisfies the conscience of the sinner. The blood of Jesus Christ cleanses from all sin (1 John 1:7) by removing guilt and thus producing a peace which passes all understanding. When the soul sees that Christ bore his sins upon the cross and endured the penalty which he had incurred, that all the demands of the law are fully satisfied, that God is more honored in his pardon than in his condemnation, that all the ends of punishment are accomplished by the work of Christ in a far higher degree than they could be by the death of the sinner, and that he has a right to plead the infinite merit of the Son of God at the bar of divine justice, then he is satisfied. Then he has peace. He is humble; he does not lose his sense of personal demerit, but the conscience ceases to demand satisfaction. Criminals have often been known to give themselves up to justice. They could not rest until they were punished. The infliction of the penalty incurred gave them peace. This is an element in Christian experience. The convinced sinner never finds peace until he lays his burden of sin on the Lamb of God; until he apprehends that his sins have been punished, as the Apostle says (Romans 8:3), in Christ.

Again, we are said to be reconciled to God by the death of his Son (Romans 5:10). But pardon does not produce reconciliation. A pardoned criminal may be restored to his civil rights, so far as the penalty remitted involved their forfeiture, but he is not reconciled to society. He is not restored to its favor. Justification, however, does secure a restoration to the favor and fellowship of God. We become the sons of God by faith in Jesus Christ (Galatians 3:26). No one can read the eighth chapter of the epistle to the Romans without being convinced that in Paul's apprehension a justified believer is something more than a pardoned criminal. He is a man whose salvation is secure because he is free from the law and all its demands; because the righteousness of the law (*i.e.,* all its righteous requirements) has been fulfilled in him, because thereby he is so united to Christ as to become a partaker of his life, because no one can lay anything to the charge of those for whom Christ died and whom God has justified, and because such believers being justified are revealed as the objects of the mysterious, immutable, and infinite love of God.

Again, justification includes or conveys a title to eternal life. Pardon is purely negative. It simply removes a penalty. It confers no title to benefits not previously enjoyed. Eternal life, however, is suspended on the positive condition of perfect obedience. The merely pardoned sinner has no such obedience. He is destitute of what, by the immutable principles of the divine government, is the indispensable condition of eternal life. He has no title to the inheritance promised to the righteous. This is not the condition of the believer. The merit of Christ is entitled to the reward. And the believer, being partaker of that merit, shares in that title. This is constantly recognized in the Scriptures. By faith in Christ we become the sons of God. But sonship involves heirship, and heirship involves a title to the inheritance. "If children, then heirs; heirs of God, and joint heirs with Christ" (Romans 8:17). This is the doctrine taught in Romans 5:12-21. For the offense of one, judgment passed on all men to condemnation. For the righteousness of one, the sentence of justification of life has passed on all; that is, of a justification which entitles to life. As the sin of Adam was the judicial ground of our condemnation (*i.e.*, was the ground on which justice demanded condemnation), so the righteousness of Christ is the judicial ground of justification. That is, it is the ground on which the life promised to the righteous should in justice be granted to the believer. The Church in all ages has recognized this truth. Believers have always felt that they had a title to eternal life. For this they have praised God in the loftiest strains. They have ever regarded it as intuitively true that Heaven must be merited. The only question was whether that merit was in them or in Christ. Being in Christ, it was a free gift to them; and thus righteousness and peace kissed each other. Grace and justice unite in placing the crown of righteousness on the believer's head.

It is no less certain that the consequences attributed to justification do not flow from the infusion of righteousness. The amount of holiness possessed by the believer does not give him peace. Even perfect holiness would not remove guilt. Repentance does not atone for the crime of murder. It does not still the murderer's conscience, nor does it satisfy the sense of justice in the public mind. It is the πρῶτον ψεῦδος of Romanism, and of every theory of subjective justification, that they make nothing of guilt, or reduce it to a minimum. If there were no guilt, then infusion of righteousness would be all that is necessary for salvation. But if there be justice in God, then no amount of holiness can atone for sin, and justification cannot consist in making the sinner holy.

Besides this, even admitting that the past could be ignored–that the guilt which burdens the soul could be overlooked or so easily removed–subjective righteousness, or holiness, is so imperfect that it could never give the believer peace. Let the holiest of men look within himself and say whether what he sees there satisfies his own conscience. If not, how can it satisfy God? He is greater than our hearts, and knows all things. No man, therefore, can have peace with God founded on what he is or on what he does. Romanists admit that nothing short of perfect holiness justifies or gives peace to the soul. In answer to the Protestant argument founded on that admission, Bellarmin says:

> Hoc argumentum, si quid probat, probat justitiam actualem non esse perfectam: non autem probat, justitiam habitualem, qua formaliter justi sumus, . . . non esse ita perfectam, ut absolute, simpliciter, et proprie justi nominemur, et simus. Non enim formaliter justi sumus opere nostro, sed opere Dei, qui simul maculas peccatorum tergit, et habitum fidei, spei, et caritatis infundit. Dei autem perfecta sunt opera. . . . Unde parvuli baptizati, vere justi sunt, quamvis nihil operis fecerint.*

Again,

> Justitia enim actualis, quamvis aliquo modo sit imperfecta, propter admixtionem venalium delictorum,

---

* "This argument, if it proves anything, proves that actual justice is not perfect: however, it does not prove that habitual justice, because of which we are formally complete . . . is not so perfect that we are called, and are, absolutely, simply, and properly complete. For we are not formally complete by means of our labor but by God's labor, who at the same time scours the blemishes of our sins and instils the condition of faith, hope, and charity. Moreover, God's labors are perfect. . . . Whence very young children are baptized, they are truly complete, although they have done no labor."

> et egeat quotidiana remissione peccati, tamen non
> propterea desinit esse vera justitia, et suo etiam quodam
> modo perfecta.*

No provision is made in this system for guilt. If the soul is made holy by the infusion of habits, or principles, of grace, it is just in the sight of God. No guilt or desert of punishment remains. "Reatus," says Bellarmin, ". . . est relatio,"† but if the thing of which it is a relation be taken away, where is the relation? It is impossible that such a view of justification can give peace. It makes no provision for the satisfaction of justice, and places all our hopes upon what is within, which our conscience and the Scripture testify cannot meet the just requirements of God.

Neither can the theory of subjective justification account for reconciliation with God, and for the same reasons. What is infused, the degree of holiness imparted, does not render us the objects of divine complacency and love. His love to us is of the nature of grace: love for the unlovely. We are reconciled to God by the death of his Son. That removes the obstacle arising from justice to the outflow toward us of the mysterious, unmerited love of God. We are accepted in the beloved. We are not in ourselves fit for fellowship with God. And if driven to depend on what is within, on our subjective righteousness, instead of peace we should have despair.

Again, justification according to the Scriptures gives a title to eternal life. For this our own righteousness is utterly inadequate. So far from anything in us being meritorious or entitled to reward, the inward state and the exercises of the holiest of men come so far short of perfection as to merit condemnation. In us there is no good thing. When we would do good, evil is present with us. There is ever a law in our members warring against the law of the mind.

---

* "For actual justice, although it is by all means imperfect because of a mixture of venal faults, and although it is without a daily remission of sin, nevertheless it does not as a result of this necessarily cease to be true justice, and even perfect in its own certain way."

† "The state of being accused . . . is relative."

Indwelling sin remains. It forced even Paul to cry out, "O wretched man that I am! Who shall deliver me from the body of this death?" (Romans 7:24). "Nullum unquam exstitisse pii hominis opus, quod, si severo Dei judicio examinaretur, non esset damnabile."* Ignoring the plain truth of Scripture and of Christian experience expressing itself in daily and hourly confession, humiliation, and prayers for forgiveness, the doctrine of subjective justification assumes that there is no sin in the believer—or no sin which merits the condemnation of God—but on the contrary that there is in him what merits eternal life. The Romanists make a distinction between a first and second justification. The first they admit to be gratuitous, and to be founded on the merit of Christ, or rather, to be gratuitously bestowed for Christ's sake. This consists in the infusion of habitual grace (*i.e.,* regeneration). This justifies in rendering the soul subjectively just or holy. The second justification is not a matter of grace. It is founded on the merit of good works, the fruits of regeneration. But if these fruits are, as our consciousness and the Scripture testify, defiled by sin, how can they merit eternal life? How can they cancel the handwriting which is against us? How can they be the ground of Paul's confident challenge, "Who shall lay anything to the charge of God's elect?" It is not what is within us, but what is without us; not what we are or do, but what Christ is and has done that is the ground of confidence and of our title to eternal life. This is the admitted doctrine of the Protestant Reformation.

> Apud theologos Augustanæ confessionis extra controversiam positum est totam justitiam nostram extra nos, et extra omnium hominum merita, opera, virtutes atque dignitatem quærendam, eamque in solo Domino nostro, Jesu Christo consistere.†

---

* "No labor of a pious man has ever appeared which, if it were considered by God's stern judgment, would not be able to be condemned" (Calvin, *Institutio,* III, xiv, 11; Berlin edition, 1834, part II, p. 38).

† "Among theologians of the Augustinian confession it has been regarded beyond dispute that our entire righteousness resides beyond us, and beyond the merits, labors, virtues and sought-after worth of all men, and that it resides only in our Lord Jesus Christ" (*Solida Declaratio,* III, 55; Hase, *Libri Symbolici,* 3d edition, Leipzig, 1846, p. 695).

As high as the heavens are above the Earth, so high is a hope founded on the work of Christ for us, above a hope founded on the merit of anything wrought in us. Calvin teaches the same doctrine as Luther.* He quotes Lombard as saying that our justification in Christ may be interpreted in two ways:

> Primum, mors Christi nos justificat, dum per eam excitatur caritas in cordibus nostris, qua justi efficimur: deinde quod per eandem exstinctum est peccatum; quo nos captivos distinebat diabolus, ut jam non habeat unde nos damnet.†

To which Calvin replies,

> Scriptura autem, quem de fidei justitia loquitur, longe alio nos ducit: nempe ut ab intuitu operum nostrorum aversi, in Dei misericordiam ac Christi perfectionem, tantum respiciamus. . . . Hic est fidei sensus, per quem peccator in possessionem venit suæ salutis, dum ex Evangelii doctrina agnoscit Deo se reconciliatum: quod intercedente Christi justitia, impetrata peccatorum remissione, justificatus sit: et quanquam Spiritu Dei regeneratus, non in bonis operibus, quibus incumbit, sed sola Christi justitia repositam sibi perpetuam justitiam cogitat.**

---

* *Institutio,* III, xi, 15, 16; *ut supra,* p. 17.

† "First, the death of Christ justifies us, while through that death love is aroused in our hearts, by which we are made complete; then, because through that same death sin is obliterated, whereby the devil divides us as captives, so that now he does not have that with which he condemns us."

** "However, the Scripture, which speaks about the justice of faith, leads us far in another direction: to be sure, so that we, having been turned away from consideration of our labors, depend so much on God's mercy and Christ's perfection. . . . This is the knowledge of faith, through which the sinner comes into possession of his own salvation, while he understands from the Evangelical docrine that he has been reconciled to God: because when he has obtained remission of his sins, and Christ's righteousness has intervened, he is justified: and although reborn in the Spirit of God, he thinks that eternal righteousness is in store for him, not in the good labors to which he applies himself, but because of Christ's justice alone."

Summary

That justification is not merely pardon, and that it is not the infusion of righteousness whereby the sinner is made inherently just or holy, but a judgment on the part of God that the demands of the law in regard to the believer are satisfied, and that he has a right to a righteousness which entitles him to eternal life has been argued:

(1) From the uniform usage of Scripture both in the Old and New Testament.

(2) From the constant opposition between justification and condemnation.

(3) From equivalent forms of expression.

(4) From the whole design and drift of the Apostle's argument in his epistles to the Romans and to the Galatians.

(5) From the ground of justification, namely, the righteousness of Christ.

(6) From the immutability of the law and the justice of God.

(7) From the nature of our union with Christ.

(8) From the fact that peace, reconciliation with God, and a title to eternal life which, according to Scripture, are the consequences of justification, do not flow either from mere pardon, or from subjective righteousness, or from sanctification.

That this is the doctrine of Protestants, both Lutheran and Reformed, cannot with any show of reason be disputed.

Calvin's Doctrine

It is true indeed that by the earlier Reformers, and especially by Calvin, justification is often said to consist in the pardon of sin. But that statement was not intended as a denial of the judicial character of justification, or as excluding the imputation of the righteousness of Christ by which the believer is counted just in the sight of the law. This is obvious from the nature of the controversy in which those Reformers were engaged. The question between them and the Romanists was, Does justification consist in the act of God making the sinner inherently just or holy? or, Does it express the judgment of God by which the believer is pronounced just? What Calvin denied was that justification is a making holy. What he affirmed was that it was delivering the believer from the condemnation of the law and introducing him into a state of favor with God. The Romanists expressed their doctrine by saying that justification consists in the remission of sin and the infusion of charity or righteousness. But by the remission of sin they meant the removal of sin, the putting off the old man. In other words, justification with them consisted (to use the scholastic language then in vogue) in the removal of the habits of sin and the infusion of habits of grace. In those justified, therefore, there was no sin, and, therefore, nothing to punish. Pardon, therefore, followed as a necessary consequence. It was a mere accessory. This view of the matter makes nothing of guilt, nothing of the demands of justice.

Calvin, therefore, insisted that besides the subjective renovation connected with the sinner's conversion, his justification concerned the removal of guilt, the satisfaction of justice, which in the order of nature–although not of time–must precede the communication of the life of God to the soul. That Calvin did not differ from the other Reformers and the whole body of the Reformed Church on this subject appears from his own explicit declarations and from the perfectly unambiguous statements of the confessions to which he gave his assent. Thus he says,

> Porro ne impingamus in ipso limine (quod fieret si de re incognita disputationem ingrediremur) primum explicemus quid sibi velint istæ loquutiones, Hominem coram Deo justificari, Fide justificari, vel operibus. Justificari coram Deo dicitur qui judicio Dei et censetur justus, et acceptus est ob suam justitiam: siqui dem ut Deo abominabilis est iniquitas, ita nec peccator in ejus

oculis potest invenire gratiam, quatenus est peccator, et quamdiu talis censetur. Proinde ubicunque peccatum est, illic etiam se profert ira et ultio Dei. Justificatur autem qui non loco peccatoris, sed justi habetur, eoque nomine consistit coram Dei tribunali, ubi peccatores omnes corruunt. Quemadmodum si reus innocens ad tribunal æqui judicis adducatur, ubi secundum innocentiam ejus judicatum fuerit, justificatus apud judicem dicitur: sic apud Deum justificatur, qui numero peccatorum exemptus, Deum habet suæ justitiæ testem et assertorem. Justificari, ergo, operibus ea ratione dicetur, in cujus vita reperietur ea puritas ac sanctitas quæ testimonium justitiæ apud Dei thronum mereatur: seu qui operum suorum integritate respondere et satisfacere illius judicio queat. Contra, justificabitur ille fide, qui operum justitia exclusus, Christi justitiam per fidem apprehendit, qua vestitus in Dei conspectu non ut peccator, sed tanquam justus apparet. Ita nos justificationem simpliciter interpretamur acceptionem, qua nos Deus in gratiam receptos pro justos habet. Eamque in peccatorum remissione ac justitiæ Christi imputatione positam esse dicimus.*

---

* "Further, so that we not block the entrance itself (which happens if we begin a debate about an unknown matter), first let us explain what those expressions signify, that man is justified in the presence of God, that he is justified either by faith or by works. He who is both considered just in God's judgment and accepted on account of his righteousness is said to be justified in the presence of God. As iniquity is hateful to God, so is a sinner unable to find grace in his eyes, insofar as he is a sinner, and as long as he is considered such. Consequently, wherever there is sin, there also the anger and vengeance of God reveals itself. However, he is justified who is held in a position not of sin but of righteousness, and in that name he stands in the presence of God's tribunal, where all sinners are thrown down. In this manner, if an innocent defendant is led to the tribunal of a just judge, he is said to be justified in the presence of the judge. So is he, who has been freed from the number of sinners, justified before God; he has God as a witness and protector of his righteousness. Therefore, he will be said to be justified, by reason of works, in whose life will be found that purity and sanctity which merits the proof of justice at God's throne: or he who can answer with the righteousness of his own works and prove them sufficiently to his judge. On the other hand, that man who, having been excluded from the righteousness of his

This passage is decisive as to the views of Calvin: for it is professedly a formal statement of the "Status Quæstionis" given with the utmost clearness and precision. Justification consists "in the remission of sins and the imputation of the righteousness of Christ." "He is justified in the sight of God, who is taken from the class of sinners and has God for the witness and assertor of his righteousness."

---

works, seizes the righteousness of Christ through his faith, he will be justified by means of faith, as far as he appears in the sight of God clothed not as a sinner but just as if perfect. Thus we interpret *justification* simply as acceptance, whereby God considers us perfect when we have been received in grace. And we say that this grace has been offered because of the remission of sins and the imputation of Christ's righteousness" (*Institutio*, III, xi, 2, *ut supra*, p. 6).

6

WORKS NOT THE GROUND OF
JUSTIFICATION

In reference to men since the Fall the assertion is so explicit and so often that justification is not of works, that that proposition has never been called into question by anyone professing to receive the Scriptures as the Word of God. It being expressly asserted that the whole world is guilty before God, that by the works of the law no flesh living can be justified, the only question open for discussion is, What is meant by works of the law?

To this question the following answers have been given: First, that by works of the law are meant works prescribed in the Jewish law. It is assumed that as Paul's controversy was with those who taught that unless men were circumcised and kept the law of Moses, they could not be saved (Acts 15:1, 24), all he intended to teach was the reverse of that proposition. He is to be understood as saying that the observance of Jewish rites and ceremonies is not essential to salvation; that men are not made righteous or good by external ceremonial works, but by works morally good. This is the ground taken by Pelagians and by most of the modern Rationalists.

It is only a modification of this view that men are not justified, that is, that their character before God is not determined, so much by their particular acts or works as by their general disposition and controlling principles. To be justified by faith, therefore, is to be justified on the ground of our trust or pious confidence in

God and truth. Thus Wegscheider says:

> Homines non singulis quibusdam recte factis operibusque operatis, nec propter meritum quoddam iis attribuendum, sed sola vera fide, *i.e.,* animo ad Christi exemplum ejusdemque præcepta composito et ad Deum et sanctissimum et benignissimum converso, ita, ut omnia cogitata et facta ad Deum ejusque voluntatem sanctissimam pie referant, Deo vere probantur et benevolentiæ Dei confisi spe beatitatis futuræ pro dignitate ipsorum morali iis concedendæ certissima imbuuntur.*

Steudlin expresses the same view. "All true reformation, every good act," he says, "must spring from faith, provided we understand by faith the conviction that something is right, a conviction of general moral and religious principles."† Kant says that Christ in a religious aspect is the ideal of humanity. When a man so regards him and endeavors to conform his heart and life to that ideal, he is justified by faith.** According to all these views, mere ceremonial works are excluded, and the ground of justification is made to be our own natural moral character and conduct.

Roman Catholic Doctrine

The doctrine of Romanists on this subject is much higher. Romanism retains the supernatural element of Christianity

---

* "Men are found truly good by God not by being properly engaged in certain discrete deeds and works nor because of certain worth attributed to them, but only by true faith: that is, by adapting their spirit to Christ's example and his commands, and by directing their spirit to God both most holy and most kind, so that all thoughts and actions answer to God and his most holy will; and they are steeped, having complete faith in God's benevolence, with hope for future blessedness for the most certain moral worth granted to them" (*Institutiones Theologiæ,* III, iii, §155, 5th edition, Halle, 1826, p. 476).

† *Dogmatik, Zweiter Theil,* §134, B, g, h; Göttingen, 1800, pp. 783, 784.

** See Strauss, *Dogmatik,* Tübingen and Stuttgart, 1841, Vol. II, pp. 493, 494.

throughout.* On the matter of justification the Romish theologians have marred and defaced the truth as they have almost all other doctrines pertaining to the mode in which the merits of Christ are made available to our salvation. They admit, indeed, that there is no good in fallen man; that he can merit nothing and claim nothing on the ground of anything he is or can do of himself. He is by nature dead in sin; and until made partaker of a new life by the supernatural power of the Holy Ghost, he can do nothing but sin. For Christ's sake, and only through his merits, as a matter of grace, this new life is imparted to the soul in regeneration *(i.e.,* as Romanists teach, in baptism). As life expels death; as light banishes darkness, so the entrance of this new divine life into the soul expels sin *(i.e.,* sinful habits) and brings forth the fruits of righteousness. Works done after regeneration have real merit, "meritum condigni [condign merit]," and are the ground of the second justification; the first justification consisting in making the soul inherently just by the infusion of righteousness. According to this view, we are not justified by works done before regeneration, but we are justified for gracious works, *i.e.,* for works which spring from the principle of divine life infused into the heart. The whole ground of our acceptance with God is thus made to be what we are and what we do.

---

* Hodge errs when he writes: "Indeed it is a matter of devout thankfulness to God that underneath the numerous grievous and destructive errors of the Romish Church, the great truths of the Gospel are preserved. The Trinity, the true divinity of Christ, the true doctrine concerning his person as God and man in two distinct natures and one person forever, salvation though his blood, regeneration and sanctification through the almighty power of the Spirit, the resurrection of the body, and eternal life, are doctrines on which the people of God in that communion live, and which have produced such saintly men as St. Bernard, Fénélon, and doubtless thousands of others who are of the number of God's elect. Every true worshipper of Christ must in his heart recognize as a Christian brother, wherever he may be found, anyone who loves, worships, and trusts the Lord Jesus Christ as God manifest in the flesh and the only Saviour of men." Hodge errs because any man or church which denies justification by faith alone cannot be said to preserve the great truths of the Gospel. Furthermore, Rome, while retaining the Biblical words, changes the meaning of the words. Modernism was not the first movement in the church to equivocate and thereby deny the truth.–*Editor.*

Arminian Doctrine

According to the Remonstrants or Arminians the works which are excluded from our justification are works of the law as distinguished from works of the Gospel. In the covenant made with Adam God demanded perfect obedience as the condition of life. For Christ's sake, God in the Gospel has entered into a new covenant with men, promising them salvation on the condition of evangelical obedience. This is expressed in different forms. Sometimes it is said that we are justified on account of faith. Faith is accepted in place of that perfect righteousness demanded by the Adamic law. But by faith is not meant the act of receiving and resting upon Christ alone for salvation. It is regarded as a permanent and controlling state of mind. And therefore it is often said that we are justified by a "fides obsequiosa," an obedient faith; a faith which includes obedience. At other times, it is said that we are justified by evangelical obedience, *i.e.,* that kind and measure of obedience which the Gospel requires, and which men since the Fall, in the proper use of "sufficient grace" granted to all men, are able to render. Limborch says, "Sciendum, quando dicimus, nos fide justificari, nos non excludere opera, quæ fides exigit et tanquam fœcunda mater producit; sed ea includere."*

And again,

> Est itaque [fides] talis actus, qui, licet in se spectatus perfectus nequaquam sit, sed in multis deficiens, tamen a Deo, gratiosa et liberrima voluntate, pro pleno et perfecto acceptatur, et propter quem Deus homini gratiose remissionem peccatorum et vitæ æternæ premium conferre vult.†

---

* "It must be known that when we say that we are justified by means of faith, we do not exclude works that faith demands, just as a fruitful mother brings forth; but we include them."

† "And so it [faith] is such an act, which although having been seen is by no means perfect in itself, but failing in many things, nevertheless is accepted as full and complete by God, because of his favorable and very unrestrained will, and because of which God graciously wishes to attribute to man remission of sins and the reward of eternal life."

Again, **God, he** says, demands, "obedientiam fidei, hoc est, non rigidam **et ab omnibus** æqualem, prout exigebat lex; sed tantam, quantam fides, id est, certa de divinis promissionibus persuasio, in unoquoque efficere potest."*
Therefore justification, he says, "est gratiosa æstimatio, seu potius acceptatio justitiæ nostræ imperfectæ pro perfecta, propter Jesum Christum."†

Protestant Doctrine

According to the doctrine of the Lutherans and Reformed, the works excluded from the ground of our justification are not only ritual or ceremonial works, nor merely works done before regeneration, nor the perfect obedience required by the law given to Adam, but works of all kinds, everything done by us or wrought in us. That this is the doctrine of the Bible is plain because the language of Scripture is unlimited. The declaration is that we are not justified "by works." No specific kind of works is designated to the exclusion of all others. But it is "works"; what we do; anything and everything we do. It is, therefore, without authority that any man limits these general declarations to any particular class of works.

The word *law* is used in a comprehensive sense. It includes all revelations of the will of God as the rule of man's obedience; and, therefore, by "works of the law" must be intended all kinds of works. As νόμος means that which binds, it is used for the law of nature, or the law written on the heart (Romans 2:14), for the Decalogue, for the law of Moses, for the whole of the Old Testament Scriptures (Romans 3:19). Sometimes one and sometimes another of these aspects of the law is specially referred to. Paul assures the Jews that they could not be justified by the works of

---

* "the obedience of faith; that is, not strict and equal obedience from all, just as the law demands, but only as much as faith, that is, a certain conviction about divine promises, can produce in each man" (*Theologia Christiana,* VI, iv, 32, 31, 37; Amsterdam edition, 1725, pp. 705, b, a, 706, a).

† "is a favorable valuation, or rather acceptance of our imperfect righteousness as perfect, because of Jesus Christ" (Limborch, VI, vi, 18; *ut supra,* p. 703, 1).

the law, which was especially binding on them. He assures the Gentiles that they could not be justified by the law written on their hearts. He assures believers under the Gospel that they cannot be justified by works of the law binding on them. The reason given includes all possible works. That reason is that all human obedience is imperfect; all men are sinners; and the law demands perfect obedience (Galatians 3:10). Therefore, it is that "by the deeds of the law there shall no flesh be justified" (Romans 3:20).

The law of which Paul speaks is the law which says, "You shall not covet" (Romans 7:7); the law which is spiritual (verse 14); which is "holy, and just, and good" (verse 12); the law of which the great command is, You shall love the Lord your God with all your heart, and your neighbor as yourself. Besides, what are called works of the law are in Titus 3:5 called "works of righteousness." Higher works than these there cannot be. The Apostle repudiates any ground of confidence in his "own righteousness" (Philippians 3:9), *i.e.,* own excellence, whether habitual or actual. He censures the Jews because they went about to establish their own righteousness and would not submit to the righteousness of God (Romans 10:3). From these and many similar passages it is clear that it is not any one or more specific kinds of work which are excluded from the ground of justification, but all works, all personal excellence of every kind.

This is still further evident from the contrast constantly presented between faith and works. We are not justified by works, but by faith in Jesus Christ (Galatians 2:16, and often elsewhere). It is not one kind of works as opposed to another; legal as opposed to evangelical; natural as opposed to gracious; moral as opposed to ritual; but works of every kind as opposed to faith.

The same is evident from what is taught of the gratuitous nature of our justification. Grace and works are antithetical. "To him that works the reward is not reckoned of grace, but of debt" (Romans 4:4). "If by grace, then is it no more of works: otherwise grace is no more grace" (Romans 11:6). Grace of necessity excludes works of every kind, and more especially those of the highest kind, which might have some show of merit. But merit of any degree is of necessity excluded, if our salvation be by grace.

When the positive ground of justification is stated, it is always declared to be not anything done by us or wrought in us, but what was done for us. It is ever represented as something external to ourselves. We are justified by the blood of Christ (Romans 5:9); by his obedience (Romans 5:19); by his righteousness (verse 18). This is involved in the whole method of salvation. Christ saves us as a priest, but a priest does not save by making those who come to him good. He does not work in them, but for them. Christ saves us by a sacrifice; but a sacrifice is effectual, not because of its subjective effect upon the offerer, but as an expiation, or satisfaction to justice. Christ is our Redeemer; he gave himself as a ransom for many. But a ransom does not infuse righteousness. It is the payment of a price. It is the satisfaction of the claims of the captor upon the captive. The whole plan of salvation, therefore–as presented in the Bible and as it is the life of the Church–is changed, if the ground of our acceptance with God be transferred from what Christ has done for us to what is wrought in us or done by us. The Romish theologians do not agree exactly as to whether habitual or actual righteousness is the ground of justification. Bellarmin says it is the former.* He says,

> Solam esse habitualem justitiam, per quam formaliter justi nominamur, et sumus: justitiam vero actualem, id est, opera vere justa justificare quidem, ut sanctus Jacobus loquitur, cum ait cap. 2 ex operibus hominem justificari, sed meritorie, non formaliter.†

---

* De Justificatione, II, 15; Disputationes, Paris edition, 1608, Vol. IV, p. 820, a.

† "It is only through habitual righteousness that we are called formally perfect, and we are: but actual righteousness, that is, truly just labors, does indeed justify, as Saint James says when he says in chapter 2 that man is justified from his labors, but deservedly, not formally."

This he says is clearly the doctrine of the Council of Trent, which teaches, "Causam formalem justificationis esse justitiam, sive caritatem, quam Deus unicuique propriam infundit, secundum mensuram dispositionum, et quæ in cordibus justificatorum inhæret."* This follows also, he argues, from the fact that the sacraments justify "per modum instrumenti ad infusionem justitiæ habitualis."† This, however, only amounts to the distinction, already referred to, between the first and second justification. The infusion of righteousness renders the soul inherently righteous; then good works merit salvation. The one is the formal, the other the meritorious cause of the sinner's justification. But according to the Scriptures, both habitual and actual righteousness, both inherent grace and its fruits are excluded from any share in the ground of our justification.

That justification is by faith alone still further and most decisively appears from the grand objection to his doctrine which Paul was constantly called upon to answer. That objection was that if our personal goodness or moral excellence is not the ground of our acceptance with God, then all necessity of being good is denied, and all motive to good works is removed. We may continue in sin that grace may abound. This objection has been reiterated a thousand times since it was urged against the Apostles. It seems so unreasonable and so demoralizing to say, as Paul says in Romans 3:22, that so far as justification is concerned there is no difference between Jew and Gentile, between a worshipper of the true God and a worshipper of demons, between the greatest sinner and the most moral man in the world that men have ever felt that they were doing God service in denouncing this doctrine as a soul-destroying heresy.

Had Paul taught that men are justified for their good moral works as the Pelagians and Rationalists say; or for their evangeli-

---

* "The formal condition of justificaton is righteousness, or charity, which God administers to each man as his own, following a measure of arrangements, and which cleaves to the hearts of the righteous" (see Session vi, cap. 7).

† "by the instrumental means of the infusion of habitual justice" (Bellarmin, *ut supra*, p. 820, b).

cal obedience as the Arminians say; or for their inherent righteousness and subsequent good works as the Romanists say, there would have been no room for this formidable objection. Or, if through any misapprehension of his teaching the objection had been urged, how easy had it been for the Apostle to set it aside. How obvious would have been the answer, "I do not deny that really good works are the ground of our acceptance with God. I only say that ritual works have no worth in his sight, that he looks on the heart"; or, that "works done before regeneration have no real excellence or merit"; or, that "God is more lenient now than in his dealing with Adam"; that "he does not demand perfect obedience, but accepts our imperfect, well-meant endeavors to keep his holy commandments." How reasonable and satisfactory would such answers have been.

Paul, however, does not make them. He adheres to his doctrine that our own personal moral excellence has nothing to do with our justification; that God justifies the ungodly; that he receives the chief of sinners. He answers the objection indeed, and answers it effectually; but his answer supposes him to teach just what Protestants teach, that we are justified without works, not for our own righteousness, but gratuitously, without money and without price, solely on the ground of what Christ has done for us. His answer is that so far from its being true that we must be good before we can be justified, we must be justified before we can be good; that so long as we are under the curse of the law we bring forth fruit unto death; that it is not until reconciled unto God by the death of his Son that we bring forth fruit unto righteousness; that when justified by the righteousness of Christ we are made partakers of his Spirit; being justified we are sanctified; that union with Christ by faith secures not only the imputation of his righteousness to our justification, but the participation of his life unto our sanctification; so that as surely as he lives and lives unto God, so they that believe on him shall live unto God; and that none is a partaker of the merit of his death who does not become a partaker of the power of his life. We do not, therefore, he says, make void the law of God. Yea, we establish the law. We teach the only true way to become holy, although that way appears foolishness unto the wise of this world, whose wisdom is folly in the sight of God.

7

THE RIGHTEOUSNESS OF CHRIST THE GROUND OF JUSTIFICATION

The imperative question remains, How shall a man be just with God? If our moral excellence be not the ground on which God pronounces us just, what is that ground? The grand reason why such different answers are given to this question is that it is understood in different senses. The Scriptural and Protestant answer is absurd, if the question means what Romanists and others understand it to mean. If "just" means good, *i.e.*, if the word be taken in its moral, and not in its judicial sense, then it is absurd to say that a man can be good with the goodness of another, or to say that God can pronounce a man to be good who is not good. Bellarmin says an Ethiopian clothed in a white garment is not white. Curcellæus, the Arminian, says, "A man can no more be just with the justice of another than he can be white with the whiteness of another." Moehler says it is impossible that anything should appear to God other than it really is, that an unjust man should appear to him or be pronounced by him just.* All this is true in the sense intended by these writers, "The judgment of God is according to truth" (Romans 2:2). Every man is truly just whom he justifies or declares to be just. It is in vain to dispute until the "status quæstionis" be clearly determined

The word δίκαιος, "righteous," or "just," has two distinct senses, as above stated. It has a moral, and also a legal, forensic,

---

* *Symbolik*, § 14, 6th edition, Mainz, 1843, p. 139.

or judicial sense. It sometimes expresses moral character, sometimes simply a relation to law and justice. In one sense, to pronounce a man just is to declare that he is morally good. In another sense, it is to declare that the claims of justice against him are satisfied, and that he is entitled to the reward promised to the righteous. When God justifies the ungodly, he does not declare that he is godly in himself, but that his sins are expiated, and that he has a title founded in justice to eternal life. In this there is no contradiction and no absurdity. If a man under attainder appear before the proper tribunal and show cause why the attainder should in justice be reversed, and he be declared entitled to his rank, titles, and estates, a decision in his favor would be a justification. It would declare him just in the eye of the law, but it would declare nothing and effect nothing as to his moral character. In the like manner, when the sinner stands at the bar of God, he can show good reason why he cannot be justly condemned and why he should be declared entitled to eternal life.

Now the question is, "On what ground can God pronounce a sinner just in this legal or forensic sense?" It has been shown that *to justify,* according to uniform Scriptural usage, is to pronounce just in the sense stated, that it is not merely to pardon, and that it is not to render inherently righteous or holy. It has also been shown to be the doctrine of Scripture, what indeed is intuitively true to the conscience, that our moral excellence–habitual or actual–is not and cannot be the ground of any such judicial declaration. What then is the ground? The Bible and the people of God with one voice answer, "The righteousness of Christ." The ambiguity of words, the speculations of theologians, and misapprehensions may cause many of the people of God to deny in words that such is the proper answer, but it is nevertheless the answer rendered by every believer's heart. He relies for his acceptance with God, not on himself but on Christ, not on what he is or has done, but on what Christ is and has done for him.

Meaning of the Terms

By the righteousness of Christ is meant all he became, did, and suffered to satisfy the demands of divine justice and merit for his people the forgiveness of sin and the gift of eternal life. The righteousness of Christ is commonly represented as including his active and passive obedience. This distinction is Scriptural. The Bible does teach that Christ obeyed the law in all its precepts, and that he endured its penalty, and that this was done in such sense for his people that they are said to have done it. They died in him. They were crucified with him. They were delivered from the curse of the law by his being made a curse for them. He was made under the law that he might redeem those who were under the law. We are freed from the law by the body of Christ. He was made sin that we might be made the righteousness of God in him. He is the end of the law for righteousness to all them that believe. It is by his obedience that many are made righteous (Romans 5:19). We obeyed in him, according to the teaching of the Apostle in Romans 5:12-21, in the same sense in which we sinned in Adam. The active and passive obedience of Christ, however, are only different phases or aspects of the same thing. He obeyed in suffering. His highest acts of obedience were rendered in the garden and upon the cross. Hence this distinction is not so presented in Scripture as though the obedience of Christ answered one purpose and his sufferings another and a distinct purpose. We are justified by his blood. We are reconciled unto God by his death. We are freed from all the demands of the law by his body (Romans 7:4), and we are freed from the law by his being made under it and obeying it in our stead (Galatians 4:4, 5). Thus the same effect is ascribed to the death or sufferings of Christ and to his obedience, because both are forms or parts of his obedience or righteousness by which we are justified. In other words the obedience of Christ includes all he did in satisfying the demands of the law.

The Righteousness of Christ Is the Righteousness of God

The righteousness of Christ, on the ground of which the believer is justified, is the righteousness of God. It is so designated in Scripture not only because it was provided and is accepted by him; it is not only the righteousness which avails before God, but it is the righteousness of a divine person of God manifest in the flesh. God purchased the Church with his own blood (Acts 20:28). It was the Lord of glory who was crucified (1 Corinthians 2:8). He who was in the form of God and thought it not robbery to be equal with God became obedient unto death, even the death of the cross (Philippians 2:6-8). He who is the brightness of the Father's glory and the express image of his person; who upholds all things by the word of his power; whom angels worship; who is called God; who in the beginning laid the foundations of the Earth, and of whose hands the heavens are the workmanship; who is eternal and immutable, has, the Apostle teaches, by death destroyed him who has the power of death and delivered those who through fear of death (*i.e.,* of the wrath of God) were all their lifetime subject to bondage. He whom Thomas recognized and avowed to be his Lord and God was the person into whose wounded side he thrust his hand. He whom John says he saw, looked upon, and handled, he declares to be the true God and eternal life. The soul, in which personality resides, does not die when the man dies; yet it is the soul that gives dignity to the man, and which renders his life of unspeakably greater value in the sight of God and man than the life of any irrational creature. So it is not the divine nature in Christ in which his personality resides, the eternal *Logos,* that died when Christ died. Nevertheless the hypostatic union between the *Logos* and the human nature of Christ makes it true that the righteousness of Christ (his obedience and sufferings) was the righteousness of God. This is the reason why it can avail before God for the salvation of the whole world. This is the reason why the believer, when arrayed in this righteousneess, need fear neither death nor Hell. This is the reason why Paul challenges the universe to lay anything to the charge of God's elect.

8

IMPUTATION OF RIGHTEOUSNESS

The righteousness of Christ is imputed to the believer for his justification. The word *impute* is familiar and unambiguous. To impute is to ascribe to, to reckon to, to lay to one's charge. When we say we impute a good or bad motive to a man, or that a good or evil action is imputed to him, no one misunderstands our meaning. Philemon had no doubt what Paul meant when he told him to impute to him the debt of Onesimus. "Let not the king impute anything unto his servant" (1 Samuel 22:15). "Let not my lord impute iniquity unto me" (2 Samuel 19:19). "Neither shall it be imputed unto him that offers it" (Leviticus 7:18). "Blood shall be imputed unto that man; he has shed blood" (Leviticus 17:4). "Blessed is the man unto whom the Lord imputes not iniquity" (Psalm 32:2). "Unto whom God imputes righteousness without works" (Romans 4:6). God is "in Christ not imputing their trespasses unto them" (2 Corinthians 5:19).

The meaning of these and similar passages of Scripture has never been disputed. Everyone understands them. We use the word *impute* in its simple, admitted sense when we say that the righteousness of Christ is imputed to the believer for his justification.

It seems unnecessary to remark that this does not and cannot mean that the righteousness of Christ is infused into the believer, or in any way so imparted to him as to change or constitute his moral character. Imputation never changes the inward, subjective state of the person to whom the imputation is made. When sin is imputed to a man he is not made sinful; when the zeal of Phinehas was imputed to him, he was not made zealous. When you impute theft to a man, you do not make him a thief. When you impute goodness to a man, you do not make him good. So when righteousness is imputed to the believer, he does not thereby become subjectively righteous. If the righteousness be adequate, and if the imputation be made on adequate grounds and by competent authority, the person to whom the imputation is made has the right to be treated as righteous. And, therefore, in the forensic (although not in the moral or subjective sense) the imputation of the righteousness of Christ does make the sinner righteous; that is, it gives him a right to the full pardon of all his sins and a claim in justice to eternal life.

That this is the simple and universally accepted view of the doctrine as held by all Protestants at the Reformation and by them regarded as the cornerstone of the Gospel has already been sufficiently proved by extracts from the Lutheran and Reformed confessions, and has never been disputed by any candid or competent authority. This has continued to be the doctrine of both the great branches of the Protestant church, so far as they pretend to adhere to their standards. Schmid proves this by a whole catena of quotations so far as the Lutheran church is concerned.* Schweizer does the same for the Reformed church.† A few citations, therefore, from authors of a recognized representative character will suffice as to this point.

Turretin with his characteristic precision says,

> Cum dicimus Christi justitiam ad justificationem nobis imputari, et nos per justitiam illam imputatam justos esse coram Deo, et non per justitiam ullam quæ nobis inhæreat; nihil aliud volumus, quam obedientiam Christi Deo Patri nomine nostro præstitam, ita nobis a Deo donari, ut vere nostra censeatur, eamque esse

---

* *Die Dogmatik der evangelisch-lutherischen Kirche, dargestellt und aus den Quellen belegt*, third edition, Frankfort and Erlangen, 1853.

† *Die Glaubenslehre der evangelisch-reformirten Kirche dargestellt und aus den Quellen belegt*, Zürich, 1844, 1847.

unicam et solam illam justitiam propter quam, et cujus
merito, absolvamur a reatu peccatorum nostrum, et jus
ad vitam obtinemus; nec ullam in nobis esse justitiam,
aut ulla bona opera, quibus beneficia tanta
promereamur, quæ ferre possint severum judicii divini
examen, si Deus juxta legis suæ rigorem nobiscum agere
vellet; nihil nos illi posse opponere, nisi Christi meritum
et satisfactionem, in qua sola, peccatorum conscientia
territi, tutum adversus iram divinam perfugium, et
animarum nostrarum pacem invenire possumus.*

On the following page he refers to Bellarmin, who says,

Si [Protestantes hoc] solum vellent, nobis imputari
Christi merita, quia [a Deo] nobis donata sunt, et
possumus ea [Deo] Patri offere pro peccatis nostris,
quoniam Christus suscepit super se onus satisfaciendi
pro nobis, nosque Deo Patri reconciliandi, recta esset
eorum sententia.†

On this Turretin remarks,

Atqui nihil aliud volumus; Nam quod addit, nos
velle "ita imputari nobis Christi justitiam, ut per eam

---

* "When we say that Christ's righteousness is reckoned as justification to us, and
that we are complete in the presence of God through that imputed righteousness, and
not through any righteousness which is inherent in us, we wish nothing other than
that Christ's obedience shown to God the Father in our name be thus granted to us by
God, so that it is counted as truly ours, and that it is that one and only justice because
of which, and because of whose worth, we are absolved from the charge of our sins.
We maintain the right to life, not that there is any righteousness in us or any good
works by which we deserve such kindness that is able to bear the severe examination
of divine judgment, if God wishes to deal with us according to the strictness of his
own law. We are able to offer nothing to him except Christ's worth and satisfaction,
the only thing in which we, frightened by the knowledge of our sins, are able to find
safe refuge from divine wrath and peace for our souls" (*Institutio, loc.* xvi. iii. 9,
Edinburgh, 1847, Vol. II, p. 570).

† "If they [Protestants] wished for [this] alone, that Christ's merits be imputed to us,
because they have been granted to us [by God] and we can offer them to [God] the

formaliter justi nominemur et simus," hoc gratis et falso supponit, ex perversa et præpostera sua hypothesi de justificatione morali. Sed quæritur, Ad quid imputatio ista fiat? An ad justificationem et vitam, ut nos pertendimus, An vero tantum ad gratiæ internæ et justitiæ inhærentis infusionem, ut illi volunt; Id est, an ita imputentur et communicentur nobis merita Christi, ut sint causa meritoria sola nostræ justificationis, nec ulla alia detur justitia propter quam absolvamur in conspectu Dei; quod volumus; An vero ita imputentur, ut sint conditiones causæ formalis, id. justitiæ inhærentis, ut ea homo donari possit, vel causæ extrinsecæ, quæ mereantur infusionem justitiæ, per quam justificatur homo; ut ita non meritum Christi proprie, sed justitia inhærens per meritum Christi acquisita, sic causa propria et vera, propter quam homo justificatur; quod illi statuunt.*

It may be remarked in passing that according to the Protestant doctrine there is properly no "formal cause" of justification. The righteousness of Christ is the meritorious but not the formal cause of the sinner's being pronounced righteous. A formal cause

---

Father in the place of our sins, since Christ has taken the burden upon himself to apologize for us and to reconcile us to God the Father, their opinion would be correct" (*De Justificatione*, ii. 7; *Disputationes*, Paris, 1608, p. 801, b).

* "But in fact we wish for nothing else; for this causes us to wish, 'Let Christ's righteousness be so imputed to us that through it we are called, and are, formally perfect.' This he supposes false and for nothing, out of his own distorted and perverse opinon about ethical justification. But it is asked, for what is this imputation done? Whether for justification and life, as we maintain, or in truth for the infusion of internal grace and inherent righteousness, as those men wish. That is, whether Christ's merits are reckoned and shared with us in such a way that they are the sole meritorious cause of our justification, and no other justice is given that absolves us in the sight of God, which is what we want; or whether Christ's merits are in fact so reckoned that they are the conditions of the formal cause of the same inherent justification that man can be granted—for example, Christ's merits are external causes that deserve the infusion of righteousness by which man is justified. Thus it is not Christ's worth exclusively, but inherent righteousness acquired through Christ's worth that is the true and lasting cause through which man is justified; this is what those men maintain."

is that which constitutes the inherent, subjective nature of a person or thing. The formal cause of a man's being good is goodness; of his being holy, holiness; of his being wicked, wickedness. The formal cause of a rose's being red is redness; and of a wall's being white is whiteness. As we are not rendered inherently righteous by the righteousness of Christ, it is hardly correct to say that his righteousness is the formal cause of our being righteous. Owen and other eminent writers do indeed often use the expression referred to, but they take the word "formal" out of its ordinary scholastic sense.

Campegius Vitringa says:

> Tenendum est certissimum hoc fundamentum, quod justificare sit vocabulum forense, notetque in Scriptura actum judicis, quo causam alicujus in judicio justam esse declarat; sive eum a crimine, cujus postulatus est, absolvat (quæ est genuina, et maxime propria vocis significatio), sive etiam jus ad hanc, vel illam rem ei sententia addicat, et adjudicet.
>
> 17. Per justificationem peccatoris intelligimus actum Dei Patris, ut judicis, quo peccatorem credentem, natura filium iræ, neque ullum jus ex se habentem bona cœlestia petendi, declarat immunem esse ab omni reatu, et condemnatione, adoptat in filium, et in eum ex gratia confert jus ad suam communionem, cum salute æterna, bonisque omnibus cum ea conjunctis, postulandi.
>
> 27. Teneamus nullam carnem in se posse reperire et ex se producere causam, et fundamentum justificationis.
>
> 29. Quærendum igitur id, propter quod peccator justificatur, extra peccatorem in obedientia Filii Dei, quam præstitit Patri in humana natura ad mortem, imo ad mortem crucis, et ad quam præstandam se obstrinxerat in sponsione (Romans 5:19).

32. Hæc [obedientia] imputatur peccatori a Deo
judice ex gratia juxta jus sposionis, de quo ante dictum.*

Owen in his elaborate work on justification proves that the
word *to justify*–"whether the act of God toward men, or of men
toward God, or of men among themselves, or of one toward another be expressed thereby–is always used in a 'forensic' sense,
and does not denote a physical operation, transfusion, or transmu-
tation."† He thus winds up the discussion:

> Wherefore as condemnation is not the infusing of
> a habit of wickedness into him that is condemned, nor
> the making of him to be inherently wicked who was
> before righteous, but the passing a sentence upon a man
> with respect to his wickedness; no more is justification
> the change of a person from inherent unrighteousness
> to righteousness by the infusion of a principle of grace,
> but a sentential declaration of him to be righteous.**

---

* "This most certain foundation must be maintained, that justification is a legal term
and that it is written in the Scripture as the act of a judge whereby he declares that
someone's cause is just in court; whether he absolves someone of a crime of which he
has been accused (which is the genuine and most proper meaning of the word), or
whether he awards the right to this case or grants someone that matter in his sentence.

"17. By the justification of sinners we understand the action of God the Father as
judge whereby he declares that the believing sinner, by nature the son of wrath and
not holding any right for seeking heavenly goods outside himself, is immune from
every accusation and condemnation; he adopts him as his son and, out of his grace,
confers upon him the right to his communion, with eternal salvation and all goods
associated with it.

"27. Let us remember that no flesh is able to find in itself, or to produce outside
itself, the cause and the foundation of justification.

"29. Therefore, we must seek beyond the sinner for that through which the sinner
is justified, to the obedience of God's Son, which he showed the Father in a human
nature until death, even to the cross finally, and for the purpose of showing this obedience he had bound himself to a solemn promise (Romans 5:19).

"32. This [obedience] is imputed to the sinner by God the judge, out of his grace,
just as the right of the promise that was discussed earlier" (*Doctrina Christianæ
Religionis*, III, xvi. 2; Leyden, 1764. Vol. III, p. 254, ff.).

† *Justification* (Philadelphia, 1841), p. 144.

** *Ibid.*, p. 154.

The ground of this justification in the case of the believing sinner is the imputation of the righteousness of Christ. This is set forth at length.* "The judgment of the Reformed Churches herein," he says,

> is known to all and must be confessed, unless we intend by vain cavils to increase and perpetuate contentions. Especially the Church of England is in her doctrine express as to the imputation of the righteousness of Christ, both active and passive, as it is usually distinguished. This has been of late so fully manifested out of her authentic writings, that is, the "Articles of Religion" and "Books of Homilies," and other writings publicly authorized, that it is altogether needless to give any further demonstration of it.

President Edwards in his sermon on justification† sets forth the Protestant doctrine in all its fulness. "To suppose," he says,

> that a man is justified by his own virtue or obedience derogates from the honor of the Mediator and ascribes that to man's virtue that belongs only to the righteousness of Christ. It puts man in Christ's stead, and makes him his own savior, in a respect in which Christ only is the Savior: And so it is a doctrine contrary to the nature and design of the Gospel, which is to abase man and to ascribe all the glory of our salvation to Christ the Redeemer. It is inconsistent with the doctrine of the imputation of Christ's righteousness, which is a gospel doctrine. Here I would (1) Explain what we mean by the imputation of Christ's righteousness. (2) Prove the thing intended by it to be true. (3) Show that this doctrine is utterly inconsistent with the doctrine of our being justified by our own virtue or sincere obedience.
> First, I would explain what we mean by the impu-

---

* *Ibid.,* p. 187.

† Sermon IV, *Works,* New York, 1868, Vol. IV, pp. 91, 92.

tation of Christ's righteousness. Sometimes the expression is taken by our divines in a larger sense, for the imputation of all that Christ did and suffered for our redemption, whereby we are free from guilt and stand righteous in the sight of God; and so implies the imputation both of Christ's satisfaction and obedience. But here I intend it in a stricter sense, for the imputation of that righteousness or moral goodness that consists in the obedience of Christ. And by that righteousness being imputed to us is meant no other than this: that that righteousness of Christ is accepted for us and admitted instead of that perfect inherent righteousness that ought to be in ourselves. Christ's perfect obedience shall be reckoned to our account so that we shall have the benefit of it as though we had performed it ourselves: And so we suppose that a title to eternal life is given us as the reward of this righteousness.

In the same connection he asks,

Why is there any more absurdity in supposing that Christ's obedience is imputed to us than that his satisfaction is imputed? If Christ has suffered the penalty of the law for us and in our stead, then it will follow that his suffering that penalty is imputed to us, *i.e.*, that it is accepted for us, and in our stead, and is reckoned to our account as though we had suffered it. But why may not his obeying the law of God be as rationally reckoned to our account as his suffering the penalty of the law.

He then goes on to argue that there is the same necessity for the one as for the other.
Dr. Shedd says,

A second difference between the Anselmic and the Protestant soteriology is seen in the formal distinction of Christ's work into his active and his passive righteousness. By his passive righteousness is meant his expiatory sufferings, by which he satisfied the claims of justice, and by his active righteousness is meant his obedience to the law as a rule of life and conduct. It was contended by those who made this distinction that the purpose of Christ as the vicarious substitute was to meet the entire demands of the law for the sinner. But the law requires present and perfect obedience, as well as satisfaction for past disobedience. The law is not completely fulfilled by the endurance of penalty only. It must also be obeyed. Christ both endured the penalty due to man for disobedience and perfectly obeyed the law for him, so that he was a vicarious substitute in reference to both the precept and the penalty of the law. By his active obedience he obeyed the law and by his passive obedience he endured the penalty. In this way his vicarious work is complete.*

The earlier confessions of the Reformation do not make this distinction. So far as the Lutheran church is concerned, it first appears in the "Form of Concord" (A.D. 1576). Its statement is as follows:

That righteousness which is imputed to faith or to believers, of mere grace, is the obedience, suffering, and resurrection of Christ, by which he satisfied the law for us and expiated our sins. For since Christ was not only man, but truly God and man in one undivided person, he was no more subject to the law than he was to suffering and death (if his person, merely, be taken into account), because he was the Lord of the law. Hence, not only that obedience to God his father which

---

* *History of Christian Doctrine*, New York, 1863, Vol. II, p. 341.

he exhibited in his passion and death, but also that obedience which he exhibited in voluntarily subjecting himself to the law and fulfilling it for our sakes, is imputed to us for righteousness, so that God on account of the total obedience which Christ accomplished *(præstitit)* for our sake before his heavenly Father, both in acting and in suffering, in life and in death, may remit our sins to us, regard us as good and righteous, and give us eternal salvation.*

In this point the Reformed or Calvinistic standards agree.

It has already been remarked that the distinction between the active and passive obedience of Christ is, in one view, unimportant. As Christ obeyed in suffering, his sufferings were as much a part of his obedience as his observance of the precepts of the law. The Scriptures do not expressly make this distinction, as they include everything that Christ did for our redemption under the term *righteousness* or *obedience*. The distinction becomes important only when it is denied that his moral obedience is any part of the righteousness for which the believer is justified, or that his whole work in making satisfaction consisted in expiation or bearing the penalty of the law. This is contrary to Scripture and vitiates the doctrine of justification as presented in the Bible.

---

* Hase, *Libri Symbolici*, third edition, Leipzig, 1846, pp. 684-685.

9

PROOF OF THE DOCTRINE

That the Protestant doctrine as above stated is the doctrine of the Word of God appears from the following considerations:

The word δικαιόω, as has been shown, means to declare δίκαιος. No one can be truthfully pronounced δίκαιος to whom δικαιοσύνη cannot rightfully be ascribed. The sinner (*ex vi verbi*) has no righteousness of his own. God, therefore, imputes to him a righteousness which is not his own. The righteousness thus imputed is declared to be the righteousness of God, of Christ, the righteousness which is by faith. This is almost in so many words the declaration of the Bible on the subject. As the question, What is the method of justification? is a Biblical question, it must be decided exegetically and not by arguments drawn from assumed principles of reason. We are not at liberty to say that the righteousness of one man cannot be imputed to another; that this would involve a mistake or absurdity; that God's justice does not demand a righteousness such as the law prescribes as the condition of justification; that he may pardon and save as a father without any consideration, unless it be that of repentance; that it is inconsistent with his grace that the demands of justice should be met before justification is granted; that this view of justification makes it a sham, a calling a man just, when he is not just, etc. All this amounts to nothing. It all pertains to that wisdom which is foolishness with God. All we have to do is to determine (1) What is the meaning of the word *to justify* as used in Scripture? (2) On what ground does the Bible affirm that God pronounces the ungodly to be just? If the answer to these questions be what the Church in all ages, and especially the Church of the Reformation, has given, then we should rest satisfied. The Apostle in express terms says that God imputes righteousness to the sinner (Romans 4:6, 24). By *righteousness* everyone admits is meant that which makes a man righteous, that which the law demands. It does not consist in the sinner's own obedience or moral excellence, for it is said to be "without works"; and it is declared that no man can be justified on the ground of his own character or conduct. Neither does this righteousness consist in faith; for it is "of faith," "through faith," "by faith." We are never said to be justified on account of faith. Neither is it a righteousness or form of moral excellence springing from faith or of which faith is the source or proximate cause, because it is declared to be the righteousness of God—a righteousness which is revealed, which is offered, which must be acccepted as a gift (Romans 5:17). It is declared to be the righteousness of Christ—his obedience (Romans 5:19). It is, therefore, the righteousness of Christ, his perfect obedience in doing and suffering the will of God which is imputed to the believer, and on the ground of which the believer, although in himself ungodly, is pronounced righteous and therefore free from the curse of the law and entitled to eternal life.

The Apostle's Argument

All the points above stated are not only clearly affirmed by the Apostle but they are also set forth in logical order and elaborately sustained and vindicated in the epistle to the Romans. The Apostle begins with the declaration that the Gospel "is the power of God unto salvation." It is not thus divinely efficacious because of the purity of its moral precepts, nor because it brings immortality to light, nor because it sets before us the perfect example of our Lord Jesus Christ, nor because it assures us of the love of God, nor because of the elevating, sanctifying, life-giving influence by which it is attended. There is something preliminary to all this. The first and indispensable requisite to salvation is that men should be righteous before God. They are under his wrath and curse. Until justice is satisfied, until God is reconciled, there is no possibility of any moral influence being of any avail. Therefore the Apostle says that the power of the Gospel is due to the fact that "therein is the righteousness of God revealed." This cannot mean the goodness of God, for such is not the meaning of the word. It cannot in this connection mean his justice, because it is a righteousness which is "of faith," because the justice of God is revealed from Heaven and to all men, because the revelation of justice terrifies and drives away from God, because what is here called the "righteousness of God" is elsewhere contrasted with our "own righteousness" (Romans 10:3, Philippians 3:9), and because it is declared to be the righteousness of Christ (Romans 5:18) which is (Romans 5:19) explained by his "obedience" and in Romans 5:9 and elsewhere declared to be "his blood." This righteousness of Christ is the righteousness of God because Christ is God—because God has provided, revealed, and offers it, and because it avails before God as a sufficient ground on which he can declare the believing sinner righteous. Herein lies the saving power of the Gospel. The question, How shall man be just with God?, had been sounding in the ears of men from the beginning. It never had been answered. Yet it must be answered or there can be no hope of salvation. It is answered in the Gospel, and therefore the Gospel is the power of God unto salvation to everyone who believes; *i.e.,* to everyone, whether Jew or Gentile, bond or free, good or bad, who, instead of going about to establish his own righteousness, submits himself in joyful confidence to the righteousness which his God and Savior Jesus Christ has wrought out for sinners, and which is freely offered to them in the Gospel without money and without price.

This is Paul's theme, which he proceeds to unfold and establish, as has been already stated under a previous head. He begins by asserting, as indisputably true from the revelation of God in the constitution of our nature, that God is just, that he will punish sin, that he cannot pronounce him righteous who is not righteous. He then shows from experience and from Scripture–first as regards the Gentiles, then as regards the Jews–that there is none righteous, no not one, that the whole world is guilty before God. There is therefore no difference, since all have sinned.

Since the righteousness which the law requires cannot be found in the sinner nor be rendered by him, God has revealed another righteousness, "the righteousness of God" (Romans 3:21), granted to every one who believes. Men are not justified for what they are or for what they do, but for what Christ has done for them. God has set him forth as a propitiation for sin, in order that he might be just and yet the justifier of them that believe.

The Apostle teaches that such has been the method of justification from the beginning. It was witnessed by the law and the prophets. There had never, since the Fall, been any other way of justification possible for men. As God justified Abraham because he believed in the promise of redemption through the Messiah, so he justifies those now who believe in the fulfilment of that promise (Romans 4:3, 9, 24). It was not Abraham's believing state of mind that was taken for righteousness. It is not faith in the believer now–not faith as a virtue or as a source of a new life which renders us righteous. It is faith in a specific promise. Righteousness, says the Apostle, is imputed to us "if we believe on him that raised up Jesus our Lord from the dead" (Romans 4:24). Or, as he expresses it in Romans 10:9: "If you shall confess with your mouth the Lord Jesus and shall believe in your heart that God has raised him from the dead, you shall be saved."

The promise which Abraham believed is the promise which we believe (Galatians 3:14), and the relation of faith to justification, in his case, is precisely what it is in ours. He and we are justified simply because we trust in the Messiah for our salvation. Hence, as the Apostle says, the Scriptures are full of thanksgiving to God for gratuitous pardon, for free justification, for the imputation of righteousness to those who have no righteousness of their own. This method of justification, he goes on to show, is adapted to all mankind. God is not the God of the Jews only but also of the Gentiles. It secures peace and reconciliation with God (Romans 5:1-3). It renders salvation certain, for if we are saved not by what we are in ourselves, but for what Christ has done for us, we may be sure that if we are "justified by his blood, we shall be saved from wrath through him" (Romans 5:9). This method of justification, he further shows, and this only, secures sanctification, namely, holiness of heart and life. It is only those who are reconciled to God by the death of his Son that are "saved by his life" (verse 10). This idea he expands and vindicates in the sixth and seventh chapters of this epistle.

The Parallel Between Adam and Christ

Not content with this clear and formal statement of the truth that sinners can be justified only through the imputation of a righteousness not their own and that the righteousness thus imputed is the righteousness (active and passive if that distinction be insisted upon) of the Lord Jesus Christ, he proceeds to illustrate this doctrine by drawing a parallel between Adam and Christ. The former, he says, was a type of the latter. There is an analogy between our relation to Adam and our relation to Christ. We are so united to Adam that his first transgression was the ground of the sentence of condemnation being passed on all mankind, and on account of that condemnation we derive from him a corrupt nature so that all mankind descending from him by ordinary generation come into the world in a state of spiritual death. In like manner, we are so united to Christ when we believe that his obedience is the ground on which a sentence of justification passes upon all thus in him, and in consequence of that sentence they derive from him a new, holy, divine, and imperishable principle of spiritual life. These truths are expressed in explicit terms: "The judgment was by one [offense] to condemnation, but the free gift is of many offenses unto justification" (Romans 5:16). "Therefore, as by the offense of one, judgment came upon all men to condemnation; even so by the righteousness of one the free gift came upon all men unto justification of life. For as by one man's disobedience many were made sinners, so by the obedience of one shall many be made righteous" (verses 18-19).

These two great truths, namely, the imputation of Adam's sin and the imputation of Christ's righteousness, have graven themselves on the consciousness of the Church universal. They have been reviled, misrepresented, and denounced by theologians; but they have stood their ground in the faith of God's people, just as the primary truths of reason have ever retained control over the mass of men, in spite of all the speculations of philosophers. It is not meant that the truths just mentioned have always been expressed in the terms just given, but the truths themselves have been and still are held by the people of God, wherever found, among the Greeks, Latins, or Protestants. The fact that the race fell in Adam, that the evils which come upon us on account of his transgression are penal, and that men are born in a state of sin and condemnation are outstanding facts of Scripture and history and are avowed every time the sacrament of baptism is administered to an infant. No less universal is the conviction of the other great truth. It is implied in every act of saving faith which includes trust in what Christ has done for us as the ground of our acceptance with God, as opposed to anything done by us or wrought in us. As a single proof of the hold which this conviction has on the Christian consciousness, reference may be made to the ancient direction for the visitation of the sick attributed to Anselm but of doubtful authorship:

Do you believe that you cannot be saved but by the death of Christ? The sick man answers, Yes. Then let it be said unto him, Go to, then, and while your soul abides in you, put all your confidence in this death alone, place your trust in no other thing, commit yourself wholly to this death, cover yourself wholly with this alone, cast yourself wholly on this death, wrap yourself wholly in this death. And if God would judge you, say, Lord, I place the death of our Lord Jesus Christ between me and your judgment, and otherwise I will not contend or enter into judgment with you. And if he shall say unto you that you are a sinner, say, I place the death of our Lord Jesus Christ between me and my sins. If he shall say unto you that you have deserved damnation, say, Lord, I put the death of our Lord Jesus Christ between you and all my sins and I offer his merits for my own, which I should have, and have not. If he say that he is angry with you, say, Lord, I place the death of our Lord Jesus Christ between me and your anger.*

Such being the real and only foundation of a sinner's hope toward God, it is of the last importance that it should not only be practically held by the people, but that it should also be clearly presented and maintained by the clergy. It is not what we do or are, but solely what Christ is and has done that can avail for our justification before the bar of God.

Other Passages Teaching the Same Doctrine

This doctrine of the imputation of the righteousness of Christ— or, in other words, that his righteousness is the judicial ground of the believer's justification—is not only formally and argumentatively presented as in the passages cited, but it is constantly asserted or implied in the Word of God. The Apostle argues, in the fourth chapter of his epistle to the Romans, that every assertion or promise of gratuitious forgiveness of sin to be found in the Scriptures involves this doctrine. He proceeds on the assumption that

---

* See "The General Considerations," prefixed by Owen to his work on *Justification*.

God is just, that he demands a righteousness of those whom he justifies. If they have no righteousness of their own, one on just grounds must be imputed to them. If, therefore, he forgives sin, it must be that sin is covered, that justice has been satisfied. "David, also," he says, "describes the blessedness of the man unto whom God imputes righteousness without works, saying, 'Blessed are they whose iniquities are forgiven, and whose sins are covered. Blessed is the man to whom the Lord will not impute sin' " (Romans 4:6-8). Not to impute sin implies the imputation of righteousness.

In Romans 5:9 we are said to be "justified by his [Christ's] blood." In Romans 3:25 God is said to have set Christ forth as a propitiation for sin, that he (God) might be just in justifying the ungodly. As *to justify* does not mean *to pardon,* but judicially to pronounce righteous, this passage distinctly asserts that the work of Christ is the ground on whch the sentence of justification is passed. In Romans 10:3-4, he says of the Jews, "They being ignorant of God's righteousness, and going about to establish their own righteousness, have not submitted themselves unto the righteousness of God. For Chirst is the end of the law for righteousness to everyone who believes." It can hardly be questioned that the word *righteousness* (δικαιοσύνη) must have the same meaning in both members of the first of these verses. If a man's "own righteousness" is that which would render him righteous, then "the righteousness of God" in this connection must be a justifying righteousness. It is called the righteousness of God, because, as said before, he is its author. It is the righteousness of Christ. It is provided, offered, and accepted of God.

Here then are two righteousnesses: the one human, the other divine; the one valueless, the other infinitely meritorious. The folly of the Jews, and of thousands since their day, consists in refusing the latter and trusting to the former. This folly the Apostle makes apparent in the fourth verse. The Jews acted under the assumption that the law as a covenant, that is, as prescribing the conditions of salvation, was still in force, that men were still bound to satisfy its demands by their personal obedience in order to be saved, whereas Christ had made an end of the law. He had abolished it as a covenant in order that men might be justified by faith. Christ, however, has thus made an end of the law, not by merely setting it aside, but by satisfying its demands. He delivers us from its curse, not by mere pardon, but by being made a curse for us (Galatians 3:13). He redeems us from the law by being made under it (Galatians 4:4-5), and fulfilling all righteousness.

In Philippians 3:8-9 the Apostle says he "suffered the loss of all things" that he might be found in Christ, not having his "own righteousness, which is of the law, but that which is through the faith of Christ, the righteousness which is of God by faith." Here again one's own righteousness is contrasted with that which is of God. The word must have the same sense in both members. What Paul trusted to was not his own righteousness, not his own subjective goodness, but a righteousness provided for him and received by faith. De Wette (no Augustinian) on this passage says the righteousness here means "a righteousness received from God (graciously imputed) on condition of faith" ("die von Gott empfangene [aus Gnaden zugerechnete] Gerechtigkeit um des Glaubenswillen").

The Apostle says (1 Corinthians 1:30) Christ "of God is made unto us wisdom, and righteousness, and sanctification, and redemption." In this enumeration, sanctification and righteousness are distinguished. The former renders us holy; the latter renders us just, i.e., satisfies the demands of justice. As Christ is to us the source of inward spiritual life, so he is the giver of that righteousness which secures our justification. Justification is not referred to sanctification as its proximate cause and grounds. On the contrary, the gift of righteousness precedes that of sanctification. We are justified in order that we may be sanctified. The point here, however, is that righteousness is distinguished from anything and everything in us which can recommend us to the favor of God. We are accepted, justified, and saved, not for what we are, but for what he has done in our behalf. God "made him to be sin for us, who knew no sin; that we might be made the righteousness of God in him" (2 Corinthians 5:21). As Christ was not made sin in a moral sense, so we are not (in justification) made righteous in a moral sense. As he was made sin in that he "bore our sins'" so we are made righteousness in that we bear his righteousness. Our sins were the judicial ground of his humiliation under the law and of all his sufferings; so his righteousness is the judicial ground of our justification. In other words, as our sins were imputed to him, so his righteousness is imputed to us. If imputation of sin did not render him morally corrupt, the imputation of righteousness does not make us holy or morally good.

Argument from the General Teaching of the Bible

It is unnecessary to dwell upon particular passages in support of a doctrine which pervades the whole Scriptures. The question is, What is the ground of the pardon of sin and of the acceptance of the believer as righteous (in the forensic or judicial sense of the word), in the sight of God? Is it anything we do, anything experienced by us or wrought in us? Or is it what Christ has done for us? The whole revelation of God concerning the method of salvation shows that it is the latter and not the former. In the first place, this is plain from what the Scriptures teach of the covenant of redemption between the Father and the Son. That there was such covenant cannot be denied if the meaning of the words be once agreed upon. It is plain from Scripture that Christ came into the world to do a certain work, on a certain condition. The promise made to him was that a multitude, whom no man can number, of the fallen race of man should be saved. This included the promise that they should be justified, sanctified, and made partakers of eternal life. The very nature of this transaction involves the idea of vicarious substitution. It assumes that what he was to do was to be the ground of the justification, sanctification, and salvation of his people.

In the second place this is involved in the nature of the work which he came to perform. He was to assume our nature, to be born of a woman, to take part of flesh and blood with all their infirmities, yet without sin. He was to take his place among sinners, be made subject to the law which they are bound to obey, and to endure the curse which they had incurred. If this be so, then what he did is the ground of our salvation from first to last: of our pardon, of our reconciliation with God, of the acceptance of our persons, of the indwelling of the Spirit, of our being transformed into his image, and of our admission into Heaven. "Not unto us, O Lord, not unto us, but unto your name give glory," has, therefore, been the spontaneous language of every believer from the beginning until now.

In the third place, the manner in which Christ was to execute the work assigned as described in the prophets, and the way in which it was actually accomplished as described by himself and by his Apostles, prove that what he did and suffered is the ground of our salvation. He says that he came "to give his life a ransom for many" (Matthew 20:28). "There is one God," says the Apostle, "and one mediator between God and men, the man Christ Jesus, who gave himself a ransom for all" (1 Timothy 2:5-6). The deliverance effected by a ransom has no reference to the character or conduct of the redeemed. Its effects are due exclusively to the ransom paid. It is, therefore, to deny that Christ was a ransom—that we are redeemed by his blood—to affirm that the proximate ground of our deliverance from the curse of the law and of our introduction into the liberty of the sons of God is anything wrought in us or done by us. Again, from the beginning to the end of the Bible, Christ is represented as a sacrifice. From the first institution of sacrifices in the family of Adam, during the patriarchal period, in all the varied and costly ritual of the Mosaic law, in the predictions of the prophets, and in the clear didactic statements of the New Testament it is taught with a constancy, a solemnity, and an amplitude which proves it to be a fundamental and vital element of the divine plan of redemption that the Redeemer was to save his people by offering himself as a sacrifice unto God in their behalf. There is no one characteristic of the plan of salvation more deeply engraven on the hearts of Christians which more effectually determines their inward spiritual life, which so much pervades their prayers and praises, or which is so directly the foundation of their hopes as the sacrificial nature of the death of Christ. Strike from the Bible the doctrine of redemption by the blood of Christ, and what have we left? But if Christ saves us as a sacrifice, then it is what he does for us–his objective work and nothing subjective, nothing in us–which is the ground of our salvation and of all that salvation includes. Even our sanctification is due to his death. His blood cleanses from all sin (1 John 1:7). It cleanses from the guilt of sin by expiation and secures inward sanctification by securing the gift of the Holy Spirit.

Again, the whole Bible is full of the idea of substitution. Christ took our place; he undertook to do for us what we could not do for ouselves. This is taught in every possible way. He bore our sins. He died for us and in our place; he was made under the law for us. He was made a curse for us. He was made sin for us that we might be made the righteousness of God in him. The chastisement of our peace was laid upon him. Everything, therefore, which the Bible teaches of the method of salvation is irreconcilable with the doctrine of subjective justification in all its forms. We are always and everywhere referred to something outside of ourselves as the ground of our confidence toward God.

In the fourth place, the effects ascribed to the work of Christ (as before remarked) are such as do not flow from anything in the believer himself, but must be referred to what has been done for him. These effects are expiation of sin; propitiation; the gift and indwelling of the life-giving Spirit of God; redemption, or deliverance from all forms of evil; and a title to eternal life and actual participation in the exaltation, glory, and blessedness of the Son of God. It is out of all question that these wonderful effects should be referred to what we personally are–to our merit, to our holiness, to our participation of the life of Christ. In whatever sense these last words may be understood, they refer to what we personally are or become. His life in us is after all a form of our life. It constitutes our character. And it is self-evident to the conscience that our character is not and cannot be the ground of our pardon, of God's peculiar love, or of our eternal glory and blessedness in Heaven.

In the fifth place, the condition on which our participation in the benefits of redemption is suspended is inconsistent with any form of the doctrine of subjective justification. We are never said to be justified on account of faith, considered either as an act or as a principle, as an exercise or as a permanent state of the mind. Faith is never said to be the ground of justification. Nor are we saved by faith as the source of holiness or of spiritual life in the soul or as the organ of receiving the infused life of God. We are saved simply "by" faith, by receiving and resting upon Christ alone for salvation. The thing received is something out of ourselves. It is Christ, his righteousness, his obedience, the merit of his blood or death. We look to him. We flee to him. We lay hold on him. We hide ourselves in him. We are clothed in his righteousness. The Romanist indeed says that an Ethiopian in a white robe does not become white. True, but a suit of armor gives security from the sword or spear, and that is what we need before attending to the state of our complexion. We need protection from the wrath of God in the first instance. The inward transformation of the soul into his likeness is provided for by other means.

In the sixth place and finally, the fact that we are saved by grace proves that the ground of salvation is not in ourselves. The grace of God, his love for the unlovely, for the guilty and polluted, is represented in the Bible as the most mysterious of the divine perfections. It was hidden in God. It could not be discovered by reason, neither was it revealed prior to the redemption of man. The specific object of the plan of salvation is the manifestation of this most wonderful, most attractive, and most glorious attribute of the divine nature. Everything connected with our salvation, says the Apostle, is intended for the "praise of the glory of his grace" (Ephesians 1:6). God has quickened us, he says, and raised us up, and made us sit together in heavenly places in Christ Jesus, in order "that in the ages to come, he might show the exceeding riches of this grace in his kindness toward us through Christ Jesus."

From their nature, grace and works are antithetical. The one excludes the other. What is of grace is not of works. And by works in Scripture, in relation to this subject, is meant not individual acts only, but states of mind, anything and everything internal of which moral character can be predicated. When, therefore, it is said that salvation is of grace and not of works, it is thereby said that it is not founded upon anything in the believer himself. It was not any moral excellence in man that determined God to interpose for his redemption, while he left the apostate angels to their fate. This was a matter of grace. To deny this and to make the provision of a plan of salvation for man a matter of justice is in such direct contradiction to everything in the Bible that it hardly ever has been openly asserted. The gift of his Son for the redemption of man is ever represented as the most wonderful display of unmerited love. That some and not all men are actually saved is expressly declared to be not of works, not on account of anything distinguishing favorably the one class from the other, but a matter of pure grace. When a sinner is pardoned and restored to the favor of God, this again is declared to be of grace. If of grace, it is not founded upon anything in the sinner himself. Now as the Scriptures not only teach that the plan of salvation is thus gratuitous in its inception, execution, and application, but also insist upon this characteristic of the plan as of vital importance, and even go so far as to teach that unless we consent to be saved by grace we cannot be saved at all, it of necessity follows that the doctrine of subjective justification is contrary to the whole spirit of the Bible. That doctrine in all its forms teaches that that which secures our acceptance with God is something in ourselves, something which constitutes character. If so, then salvation is not of grace; and if not of grace, it is unattainable by sinners.

10

THE CONSEQUENCES OF THE
IMPUTATION OF RIGHTEOUSNESS

It is frequently said that justification consists in the pardon of sin and in the imputation of righteousness. This mode of statement is commonly adopted by Lutheran theologians. This exhibition of the doctrine is founded upon the sharp distinction made in the Form of Concord between the passive and active obedience of Christ. To the former is referred the remission of the penalty due to us for sin; to the latter our title to eternal life. The Scriptures, however, do not make this distinction so prominent. Our justification as a whole is sometimes referred to the blood of Christ and sometimes to his obedience. This is intelligible because the crowning act of his obedience, and that without which all else had been unavailing, was his laying down his life for us. It is, perhaps, more correct to say that the righteousness of Christ, including all he did and suffered in our stead, is imputed to the believer as the ground of his justification, and that the consequences of this imputation are, first, the remission of sin, and secondly, the acceptance of the believer as righteous. And if righteous, then he is entitled to be so regarded and treated.

By the remission of sin, Romanists understand the removal of the pollution of sin. Their definition of *justification* as consisting in the remission of sin and infusion of righteousness is only a statement of the negative and positive aspects of sanctification, *i.e.,* putting off the old man and putting on the new man. The effect of remission is constantly declared to be that nothing of the nature of sin remains in the soul. The Council of Trent says,

> Justificatio . . . non est sola peccatorum remissio, sed et sanctificatio, et renovatio interioris hominis per voluntariam susceptionem gratiæ et donorum. . . . Quanquam nemo possit esse justus, nisi cui merita passionis Domini nostri Jesu Christi communicantur: id tamen in hac impii justificatione fit, dum ejusdem sanctissimæ passionis merito per Spiritum Sanctum caritas Dei diffunditur in cordibus eorum, qui justificantur, atque ipsis inhæret.
>
> Quibus verbis justificationis impii descriptio insinuatur, ut sit translatio ab eo statu, in quo homo nascitur filius primi Adæ, in statum gratiæ et adoptionis filiorum Dei, per secundum Adam Jesum Christum, salvatorem nostrum: quæ quidem translatio post evangelium promulgatum sine lavacro regenerationis, aut ejus voto fieri non potest.*

By "status gratiæ" in this definition is not meant a state of favor, but a state of subjective grace or holiness; because in other places and most commonly justification is said to consist in the infusion of grace. In this definition, therefore, the pardon of sin in the proper sense of the words is not included. Bellarmin says this

---

* "Justification . . . is not only a remission of sins, but also sanctification and renewal of the inner man through the voluntary undertaking of grace and gifts. . . . Although no one is able to be perfect unless the merits of our Lord Jesus Christ's suffering are conferred upon him, nevertheless this happens in the justification of a godless man, while because of the worth of the same most sacred suffering, the love of God is extended to the hearts of those who are justified through the Holy Spirit, and it cleaves to them.

"With these words is the description of a godless man's justification introduced, so that it is a change from the condition in which man is born as the son of the first Adam, to a state of grace and by adoption the sons of God, through the second Adam, our savior Jesus Christ. Indeed, since the publication of the gospel, this change cannot happen without the washing of regeneration or his will" (Sess. VI, cap. 7, 4; Streitwolf, *Libri Symbolici*, Göttingen, 1846, pp. 24, 25, 22).

translation into a state of adoption as sons of God,

> non potest . . . fieri, nisi homo per remissionem peccati desinat esse impius; et per infusionem justitiæ incipiat esse pius. Sed sicut aër cum illustratur a sole per idem lumen, quod recipit, desinit esse tenebrosus et incipit esse lucidus: sic etiam homo per eandem justitiam sibi a sole justitiæ donatam atque infusam desinit esse injustus, delente videlicet lumine gratiæ tenebras peccatorum.*

The remission of sin is therefore defined to be the removal of sin. Bellarmin argues in support of this view that guilt is removed by holiness, that guilt is a relation; the relation of sin to justice. When the thing itself is taken away, the relation itself of course ceases.† Hence remission of sin, even in the sense of pardon, is effected by the infusion of righteousness, as darkness is banished by the introduction of light. It is thus, as remarked above, that guilt is either ignored or reduced to a minimum by the Romish theory of justification. There is really no satisfaction of justice in the case. The merits of Christ avail to secure for man the gift of the Holy Ghost, by whose power as exercised in the sacrament of baptism the soul is made holy, and by the introduction of holiness everything of the nature of sin is banished, and all ground for the infliction of punishment is removed. A scheme so opposed to Scripture, and so inconsistent with even the natural conscience, cannot be practically adopted by the mass of the people. The conviction is too intimate that the desert of punishment is not removed by the reformation—or even by the regeneration—of the sinner to allow the conscience to be satisfied with any scheme of salvation which

---

* "cannot . . . happen, unless a man through remission of his sins ceases to be god-less; and through the infusion of righteousness he begins to be pious. But just as the air ceases to be dark and begins to be bright when it is lit by the sun, through the same light which it receives, so, too, does a man cease to be imperfect through that same righteousness granted to him by the sun of righteousness, namely, with the light of grace wiping out the shadow of sins" (*De Justificatione*, II, ii.; *Disputationes*, Paris, 1608, Vol. IV, pp. 780, 3, 781, a).

† *De Amissione Gratiæ et Statu Peccati*, v. vii., *ibid.*, p. 287, a, b.

does not provide for the expiation of the guilt of sin by what really satisfies the justice of God.

In the Bible, therefore, as well as in common life, pardon is not a mere consequence of sanctification. It is exemption from the infliction of the deserved penalty of the law. Whether this exemption is a mere matter of caprice, or unworthy partiality for the offender, or for considerations of expediency, or at the promptings of compassion, or upon the ground of an adequate satisfaction to the demands of justice, makes no difference so far as the nature of pardon is concerned. It is in all cases the remission of a penalty adjudged to be deserved. It is in this sense, therefore, that justification is declared to include the pardon of sins, founded on the imputation to the believing sinner of the perfect righteousness of Christ. It is this that gives the believer peace. He sees that he is delivered from "the wrath and curse of God" due to him—not by any arbitrary exercise of executive authority—but because God, as a righteous judge, can, in virtue of the propitiation of Christ, be just and yet justify the ungodly.

The sins which are pardoned in justification include all sins—past, present, and future. It does indeed seem to be a solecism that sins should be forgiven before they are committed. Forgiveness involves remission of penalty. But how can a penalty be remitted before it is incurred? This is only an apparent difficulty arising out of the inadequacy of human language. The righteousness of Christ is a perpetual donation. It is a robe which hides, or as the Bible expresses it, covers from the eye of justice the sins of the believer. They are sins; they deserve the wrath and curse of God, but the necessity for the infliction of that curse no longer exists. The believer feels the constant necessity for confession and prayer for pardon, but the ground of pardon is ever present for him to offer and plead. So that it would perhaps be a more correct statement to say that in justification the believer receives the promise that God will not deal with him according to his transgressions, rather than to say that sins are forgiven before they are committed.

This subject is thus presented by the Apostle: Believers "are not under the law but under grace" (Romans 6:14). They are not under a legal system administered according to the principles of retributive justice, a system which requires perfect obedience as the condition of acceptance with God, and which says, "Cursed is every one that continues not in all things which are written in the book of the law to do them." They are under grace, that is, under a system in which believers are not dealt with on the principles of justice, but on the principles of undeserved mercy in which God does not impute "their trespasses unto them" (2 Corinthians 5:19). There is therefore to them no condemnation. They are not condemned for their sins, not because they are not sins and do not deserve condemnation, but because Christ has already made expiation for their guilt and makes continual intercession for them.

The second consequence attributed to the imputation of Christ's righteousness is a title to eternal life. This in the older writers is often expressed by the words "adoption and heirship." Being made the children of God by faith in Christ Jesus (Galatians 2:36), they are heirs of God and joint heirs with Jesus Christ of a heavenly inheritance (Romans 8:17). The mere expiation of guilt confers no title to eternal life. The condition of the covenant under which man was placed was perfect obedience. This, from all that appears in Scripture, the perfection of God requires. As he never pardons sins unless the demands of justice be satisfied, so he never grants eternal life unless perfect obedience be rendered. Heaven is always represented as a purchased possession. In the covenant between the Father and the Son the salvation of his people was promised as the reward of his humiliation, obedience, and death. Having performed the stipulated conditions, he has a claim to the promised recompense. And this claim inures to the benefit of his people. But besides this, as the work of Christ consisted in his doing all that the law of God or covenant of works requires for the salvation of men and as that righteousness is freely offered to everyone who believes, every such believer has as valid a claim to eternal life as he would have had, had he personally done all that the law demands. Thus broad and firm is that foundation which God has laid for the hopes of his people. It is the rock of ages: Jehovah our righteousness.

11

RELATION OF FAITH TO JUSTIFICATION

All who profess to be Christians admit the doctrine of justification by faith. There are different views, however, as to the relation between faith and justification, as has been already intimated.

Pelagians and rationalists teach that faith in God's being and perfection, or in the great principles of moral and religious truth, is the source of that moral excellence on account of which we are accepted by God. It is perhaps only a different way of expressing the same idea to say that God, in the case of Abraham–and, therefore, of other men–accepts the pious state of mind involved in the exercise of faith or confidence in God, in lieu of perfect righteousness.

Romanists make faith mere assent; that is, faith does not justify as a virtue, nor as apprehending the offered righteousness of Christ. It is neither the formal nor the instrumental cause of justification; it is merely the predisposing or occasional cause. A man assents to the truth of Christianity and to the more special truth that the Roman Church is the divine institution for saving men. He therefore comes to the Roman Church and receives the sacrament of baptism, by which, "ex opere operato," a habit of grace or spiritual life is infused into the soul, which is the formal cause of justification; *i.e.,* it renders the soul inherently just or holy. In this sense the sinner may be said to be justified by faith. This is the first justification. After the man is thus rendered holy or regenerated, then the exercises of faith have real merit and enter into the ground of his second justification, by which he becomes entitled to eternal life. But here faith stands on a level with other Christian graces. It is not the only, nor the most important, ground of justification. It is in this view inferior to love, from which faith indeed derives all its virtue as a Christian grace. It is then "fides formata," *i.e.,* faith of which love is the essence, the principle which gives it character.

Roman Catholic Doctrine

According to the Romish scheme:

(1) God is the efficient cause of justification, as it is by his power or supernatural grace that the soul is made just.

(2) Christ is the meritorious cause, as it is for his sake God grants this saving grace or influence of the Spirit to the children of men.

(3) Inherent righteousness is the formal cause, since thereby the soul is made really just or holy.

(4) Faith is merely the occasional and predisposing cause, as it leads the sinner to seek justification (regeneration) and disposes God to grant the blessing. In this aspect it has the merit of congruity only, not that of condignity.

(5) Baptism is the essential instrumental cause, as it is only through or by baptism that inherent righteousness is infused or justification is effected.

So much for the first justification. After this justification, which makes the sinner holy, then,

(6) Good works, all the fruits and exercises of the new life, have real merit and constitute the ground of the Christian's title to eternal life.

The language of the Council of Trent on this subject is as follows:

> Hujus justificationis causæ sunt, finalis quidem, gloria Dei et Christi, ac vita æterna: efficiens vero, misericors Deus, qui gratuito abluit et sanctificat,

signans et ungens Spiritu promissionis sancto, . . .
meritoria autem dilectissimus unigenitus suus, Dominus
noster, Jesus Christus, qui, cum essemus inimici, propter
nimiam caritatem, qua dilexit nos, sua sanctissima
passione in ligno crucis nobis justificationem [*i.e.,* re-
generation] meruit et pro nobis Deo Patri satisfecit:
instrumentalis item, sacramentum baptismi, quod est
sacramentum fidei, sine qua nulli unquam contigit
justificatio: demum unica formalis causa est justitia Dei,
non qua ipse justus est, sed qua nos justos facit: qua
videlicet ab eo donati, renovamur spiritu mentis nostræ,
et non modo reputamur, sed vere justi nominamur, et
sumus, justitiam in nobis recipientes, unusquisque suam
secundum mensuram, quam Spiritus Sanctus partitur
singulis prout vult, et secundum propriam cujusque
dispositionem et cooperationem.*

Again, it is said: "Quæ enim justitia nostra dicitur, quia per
eam nobis inhærentem justificamur; illa eadem Dei est, quia a Deo
nobis infunditur per Christi meritum."†

---

* "The reasons for this justification are finally the glory of God and of Christ and
eternal life; but also the compassionate God, who freely washes away and sanctifies,
signifying and anointing by means of the Holy Spirit of promise. . . . Moreover, his
own most beloved only begotten son, our Lord Jesus Christ, who earned justification
[*i.e.,* regeneration] for us with his own most sacred suffering on the wooden cross,
because of his great love, whereby he loved us although we were hostile, and who
gave all that was required to God the Father on our behalf. Likewise instrumental is
the sacrament of baptism, which is a sacrament of faith, without which justification
has never touched anyone. Finally, the only formal reason is the righteousness of
God, not whereby he himself is righteous, but whereby he makes us righteous; namely,
when we have been granted this by him, we are renewed in the spirit of our mind, and
not only are we reputed to be perfect, but we are called, and are, truly perfect, receiving righteousness in ourselves, each man according to his own measure, which the
Holy Spirit distributes severally just as he wishes, and according to the characteristic
disposition and cooperation of each."

† "For this righteousness is said to be ours, since we are justified through its cleaving
to us; that same righteousness is God's, since it is poured upon us by God through
Christ's merit" (Sess. VI. cap. 7, 16; Streitwolf, *Libri Symbolici*, Göttingen, 1846,
Vol. I, pp. 24, 25, 32).

All this relates to the first justification, or regeneration, in which the soul passes from spiritual death to spiritual life. Of the second justification, which gives a title to eternal life, Bellarmin says, "Habet communis catholicorum omnium sententia, opera bona justorum vere, ac proprie esse merita, et merita non cujuscunque præmii, sed ipsius vitæ æternæ."* The thirty-second canon of the Tridentine Council at this sixth session anathematizes anyone who teaches a different doctrine:

Si quis dixerit, hominis justificati bona opera ita esse dona Dei, ut non sint etiam bona ipsius justificati merita; aut ipsum justificatum bonis operibus, quæ ab eo per Dei gratiam et Jesu Christi meritum, cujus vivum membrum est, fiunt, non vere mereri augmentum gratiæ, vitam æternam, et ipsius vitæ æternæ, si tamen in gratia decesserit, consecutionem, atque etiam gloriæ augmentum; anathema sit.†

It appears from all this that, according to the doctrine of the church of Rome, faith has no special or direct connection with justification, and that "justification by faith" in that church means something entirely different from what is intended by those words on the lips of Christians.

Arminian Doctrine

According to the Remonstrants or Arminians, faith is the ground of justification. Under the Gospel, God accepts our imper-

---

* "The common idea of all Catholic principles maintains that good works of the truly righteous are in themselves merits, and merits not of any available reward but of eternal life itself" (*De Justificatione*, v. 1; *Disputationes*, Paris, 1608, p. 949, a).

† "If anyone says that the good works of a justified man thus are gifts of God, and so not also real merits of the justified man himself; or that the justified man himself does not truly deserve an increase in grace and eternal life because of his good works, which are done by him through God's grace and the merits of Jesus Christ, whose living part he is, if nevertheless he dies in a state of grace, [that he does not truly deserve] the effect, and even an increase in glory; it is anathema."

fect obedience–including faith and the obedience springing from it–in place of the perfect obedience demanded by the law originally given to Adam. There is one passage in the Bible, or rather one form of expression that occurs in several places, which seems to favor this view of the subject. In Romans 4:3, it is said, "Abraham believed God, and it was counted unto him for righteousness"; and again in verse 22 of that chapter and in Galatians 3:6. If this phrase be interpreted according to the analogy of such passages as Romans 2:26, "Shall not his uncircumcision be counted for circumcision?" it does mean that faith is taken or accepted for righteousness. The Bible, however, is the Word of God and therefore self-consistent. Consequently, if a passage admits of one interpretation inconsistent with the teaching of the Bible in other places, and of another interpretation consistent with that teaching, we are bound to accept the latter. This rule, simple and obvious as it is, is frequently violated, not only by those who deny the inspiration of the Scriptures, but even by men professing to recognize their infallible authority. They seem to regard it as a proof of independence to make each passage mean simply what its grammatical structure and logical connection indicate, without the least regard to the analogy of Scripture. This is unreasonable. In Genesis 15, we are told that Abraham lamented before the Lord that he was childless, and that one born in his house was to be his heir. And God said unto him,

> This shall not be your heir, but he that shall come forth out of your own bowels shall be your heir. And he brought him forth abroad and said, "Look now toward Heaven and tell the stars, if you be able to number them." And he said unto him, "So shall your seed be." And he believed in the Lord, and he counted it to him for righteousness.

Taking this passage by itself, it is inferred that the object of Abraham's faith was the promise of a numerous posterity.

Supposing this to be true, which it certainly is not, what right has any one to assume that Abraham's faith's being imputed to him for righteousness means anything more than when it is said that the zeal of Phinehas was imputed for righteousness (Psalm 106:31); or when in Deuteronomy 24:13 it is said that to return a poor man's pledge "shall be righteousness unto you before the Lord your God." No one supposes that one manifestation of zeal or one act of benevolence is taken for complete obedience to the law. All that the phrase "to impute for righteousness" by itself means, according to Old Testament usage, is to esteem as right, to approve. The zeal of Phinehas was right. Returning a poor man's pledge was right. These were acts which God approved. And so he approved of Abraham's faith. He gained the favor of God by believing.

Now while this is true, far more, as the Apostle teaches, is true. He teaches, first, that the great promise made to Abraham (faith in which secured his justification) was not that his natural descendants should be as numerous as the stars of Heaven, but that in his seed all the nations of the Earth should be blessed; second, that the seed intended was not a multitude, but one person, and that that one person was Christ (Galatians 3:16); and third, that the blessing which the seed of Abraham was to secure for the world was redemption. "Christ has redeemed us from the curse of the law, being made a curse for us: . . . that the blessing of Abraham (i.e., the promise made to Abraham) might come on" us. The promise made to Abra-ham, therefore, was redemption through Christ. Hence those who are Christ's, the Apostle teaches, are Abraham's seed and heirs of his promise. What, therefore, Abraham believed was that the seed of the woman, the Shiloh, the promised Redeemer of the world, was to be born of him. He believed in Christ as his Savior, as his righteousness and deliverer; and therefore it was that he was accepted as righteous–not for the merit of his faith, and not on the ground of faith, or by taking faith in lieu of righteousness– but because he received and rested on Christ alone for his salvation.

Unless such be the meaning of the Apostle, it is hard to see how there is any coherence or force in his arguments. His object is to prove that men are justified, not by works, but gratuitously; nor for what they are or do, but for what is done for them. They are saved by a ransom, by a sacrifice. But it is absurd to say that trust in a ransom redeems or is taken in place of the ransom, or that faith in a sacrifice, and not the sacrifice itself, is the ground of acceptance. To prove that such is the Scriptural method of justification, Paul appeals to the case of Abraham. He was not justified for his works, but by faith in a Redeemer. He expected to be justified as ungodly (Romans 4:5). This, he tells us, is what we must do. We have no righteousness of our own. We must take Christ for our wisdom, righteousness, sanctification, and redemption. In the immediately preceding chapter the Apostle had said we are justified by faith in the blood of Christ as a propitiation for sin. For him to prove this from the fact that Abraham was justified on account of his confiding, trusting state of mind, which led him to believe that although a hundred years old he should be the father of a numerous posterity, would be a contradiction.

Besides, it is to be remembered not only that the Scriptures never say that we are justified "on account" of faith (διὰ πίστιν), but always "by," or "through" faith (διὰ or ἐκ πίστεως or πίστει); but also that it is not by faith as such; not by faith in God, nor in the Scriptures; and not by faith in a specific divine promise such as that made to Abraham of a numerous posterity, or of the possession of the land of Canaan; but only by faith in one particular promise, namely, that of salvation through Christ. It is, therefore, not on account of the state of mind of which faith is the evidence, nor of the good works which are its fruits, but only by faith as an act of trust in Christ, that we are justified. This of necessity supposes that he, and not our faith, is the ground of our justification. He, and not our faith, is the ground of our confidence. How can any Christian wish it to be otherwise? What comparison is there between the absolutely perfect and the infinitely meritorious righteousness of Christ and our own imperfect evangelical obedience as a ground of confidence and peace?

This doctrine of faith as the ground of our justification is, moreover, dishonoring the the Gospel. It supposes the Gospel to be less holy than the law. The law required perfect obedience; the Gospel is satisfied with imperfect obedience. And how imperfect and insufficient our best obedience is, the conscience of every believer certifies. If it does not satisfy us, how can it satisfy God?

The grand objection, however, to this Arminian doctrine as to the relation between faith and justification is that it is in direct contradiction to the plain and pervading teaching of the Word of God. The Bible teaches that we are not justified by works. This doctrine affirms that we are justified by works. The Bible teaches that we are justified by the blood of Christ–that it is for his obedience that the sentence of justification is passed on men. This doctrine affirms that God pronounces us righteous because of our own righteousness. The Bible from first to last teaches that the whole ground of our salvation or of our justification is objective: what Christ as our Redeemer, our ransom, our sacrifice, and our surety has done for us. This doctrine teaches us to look within to what we are and to what we do as the ground of our acceptance with God. It may safely be said that this is altogether unsatisfactory to the awakened conscience. The sinner cannot rely on anything in himself. He instinctively looks to Christ, to his work done for us as the ground of confidence and peace. This in the last resort is the hope of all believers, whatever their profession of justification may be. Whether Papist, Arminian, or Augustinian, they all cast their dying eyes on Christ: "As Moses lifted up the serpent in the wilderness, even so must the Son of man be lifted up–that whosoever believes in him should not perish, but have eternal life."

Protestant Doctrine

The common doctrine of Protestants on this subject is that

faith is merely the instrumental cause of justification. It is the act of receiving and resting upon Christ and has no other relation to the end than any other act by which a proffered good is accepted. This is clearly the doctrine of Scripture:

(1) Because we are constantly said to be justified by, or through, faith.

(2) Because the faith which justifies is described as a looking, as a receiving, as a coming, as a fleeing for refuge, as a laying hold of, and as a calling upon.

(3) Because the ground to which our justification is referred, and that on which the sinner's trust is placed, is declared to be the blood, the death, the righteousness, the obedience of Christ.

(4) Because the fact that Christ is a ransom, a sacrifice—and as such effects our salvation—of necessity supposes that the faith which interests us in the merit of his work is a simple act of trust.

(5) Because any other view of the case is inconsistent with the gratuitous nature of justification, with the honor of Christ, and with the comfort and confidence of the believer.

12

OBJECTIONS TO THE PROTESTANT DOCTRINE OF JUSTIFICATION

It is said to lead to licentiousness

The first, most obvious, and most persistently urged objection against the doctrine of gratuitous justification through the imputation of the righteousness of Christ has already been incidentally considered. That objection is that the doctrine leads to license: that if good works are not necessary to justification, they are not necessary at all–that if God accepts the chief of sinners as readily as the most moral of men on the simple condition of faith in Christ, then what profit is there in circumcision? in Judaism? in being in the Church? in being good in any form? Why not live in sin that grace may abound? This objection having been urged against the Apostle, it needs no other answer than that which he himself gave it. That answer is found in the sixth and seventh chapters of his epistle to the Romans and is substantially as follows:

First: the objection involves a contradiction. To speak of salvation in sin is as great an absurdity as to speak of life in death. Salvation is deliverance from sin. How then can men be delivered from sin in order that they may live in it? Or, as Paul expresses it, "How shall we, who are dead to sin, live any longer therein?"

Second, the very act of faith which secures our justification secures also our sanctification. It cannot secure the one without securing also the other. This is not only the intention and the desire of the believer, but it is the ordinance of God–a necessary feature of the plan of salvation and secured by its nature. We take Christ as our Redeemer from sin, from its power as well as from its guilt. And the imputation of his righteousness consequent on faith secures the indwelling of the Holy Spirit as certainly, and for the very same reasons (the covenant stipulations), that it secures the pardon of our sins. And, therefore, if we are partakers of his death, we are also partakers of his life. If we die with him, we rise with him. If we are justified, we are sanctified. He, therefore, who lives in sin, proclaims himself an unbeliever. He has neither part nor lot in the redemption of him who came to save his people from their sins.

Third, our condition, the Apostle says, is analogous to that of a slave, belonging first to one master, then to another. So long as he belonged to one man, he was not under the authority of another. But if freed from the one and made the slave of the other, then he comes under an influence which constrains obedience to the latter. So we were the slaves of sin, but now, freed from that hard master, we have become the servants of righteousness. For a believer, therefore, to live in sin is just as impossible as for the slave of one man to be at the same time the slave of another. We are indeed free but not free to sin. We are free only from the bondage of the devil and introduced into the pure, exalted, and glorious liberty of the sons of God.

Fourth, the objection as made against the Apostle and as constantly repeated since is urged in the interest of morality and of common sense. Reason itself, it is said, teaches that a man must be good before he can be restored to the favor of God; and if we teach that the number and heinousness of a man's sins are no barrier to his justification, and his good works are no reason why he should be justified rather than the chief of sinners, we upset the very foundations of morality. This is the wisdom of men. The wisdom of God, as revealed in the Scriptures, is very different. According to the Bible the favor of God is the life of the soul. The light of his countenance is to rational creatures what the light of the Sun is to the Earth, the source of all that is beautiful and good. So long, therefore, as a soul is under his curse, there is no life-giving or life-sustaining intercourse between it and God. In this state it can only, as the Apostle expresses it, "bring forth fruit unto death." As soon, however, as it exercises faith, it receives the imputation of the righteousness of Christ; God's justice is thereby satisfied, and the Spirit comes and takes up his dwelling in the believer as the source of all holy living. There can therefore be no holiness until there is reconciliation with God, and no reconciliation with God except through the righteousness imputed to us and received by faith alone. Then follow the indwelling of the Spirit, progressive sanctification, and all the fruits of holy living.

It may be said that this scheme involves an inconsistency. There can be no holiness until there is reconciliation, and no reconciliation until there is faith. But faith is a fruit of the Spirit, and an act of the renewed soul. Then there is and must be, after all, holy action before there is reconciliation. It might be enough to say in answer to this objection that logical order and chronological succession are different things, or that the order of nature and order of time are not to be confounded. Many things are contemporaneous and co-instantaneous which nevertheless stand in a certain logical and even causal relation to each other. Christ commanded the man with a withered arm to stretch forth his hand. He immediately obeyed, but not before he received strength. He called to Lazarus to come forth from the grave and he came forth. But this presupposes a restoration of life. So God commands the sinner to believe in Christ, and he thereupon receives him as his Savior, though this supposes supernatural power or grace.

Our Lord, however, gives another answer to this objection. He says, as recorded in John 17:9, "I pray not for the world, but for them which you have given me; for they are yours." The intercession of Christ secures for those given to him by the Father the renewing of the Holy Ghost. The first act of the renewed heart is faith; as the first act of a restored eye is to see. Whether this satisfies the understanding or not, it remains clear as the doctrine of the Bible that good works are the fruits and consequences of reconciliation with God through faith in our Lord Jesus Christ.

It is "inconsistent with the grace of the Gospel"

It is objected that the Protestant doctrine destroys the gratuitous nature of justification. If justice be satisfied, if all the demands of the law are met, there can, it is said, be no grace in the salvation of the sinner. If a man owes a debt and someone pays it for him, the creditor shows no grace in giving an acquittal. This objection is familiar, and so also is the answer.

The work of Christ is not of the nature of a commercial transaction. It is not analogous to a pecuniary satisfaction except in one point. It secures the deliverance of those for whom it is offered and by whom it is accepted. In the case of guilt the demand of justice is upon the person of the offender. He, and he alone, is bound to answer at the bar of justice. No one can take his place, unless with the consent of the representative of justice and of the substitute, as well as of the sinner himself. Among men, substitution in the case of crime and its penalty is rarely, if ever, admissible, because no man has the right over his own life or liberty. He cannot give them up at pleasure, and no human magistrate has the right to relieve the offender or to inflict the legal penalty on another. But Christ had power, *i.e.,* the right (ἐξουσία) to lay down his life and "power to take it again." And God, as absolute judge and sovereign, the Lord of the conscience and the proprietor of all his creatures, was at full liberty to accept a substitute for sinners. This is proved beyond contradiction by what God has actually done. Under the old dispensation every sacrifice appointed by the law was a substitute for him in whose behalf it was offered. In the clearest terms it was predicted that the Messiah was to be the substitute of his people–that the chastisement of their sins was to be laid on him, and that he was to make his soul an offering for sin. He was hailed as he entered on his ministry as the Lamb of God who was to bear the sins of the world. He died, the just for the unjust. He redeemed us from the curse of the law by being made a curse for us. This is what is meant by being a substitute. To deny this is to deny the central idea of the Scriptural doctrine of the redemption. To explain it away is to absorb as with a sponge the lifeblood of the Gospel.

It is the glory, the power, and the preciousness of the Protestant doctrine that it makes the salvation of sinners a matter of grace from the beginning to the end. On the part of the eternal Father it was of grace, *i.e.*, of unmerited, mysterious, and immeasurable love that he provided a substitute for sinners, and that he spared not his own Son but freely gave him up for us all. It was a matter of grace–*i.e.*, of love to sinners, to the ungodly, to his enemies– that the eternal Son of God became man, assumed the burden of our sins, fulfilled all righteousness, obeying and suffering even unto death, that we might not perish but have eternal life. It is of grace that the Spirit applies to men the redemption purchased by Christ, that he renews the heart, that he overcomes the opposition of sinners, making them willing in the day of his power; that he bears with all their ingratitude, disobedience, and resistance, and never leaves them until his work is consummated in glory. In all this the sinner is not treated according to his character and conduct. He has no claim to any one in this long catalogue of mercies. Everything to him is a matter of unmerited grace. Merited grace, indeed, is a solecism. And so is merited salvation in the case of sinners.

Grace does not cease to be grace because it is not exercised in violation of order, propriety, and justice. It is not the weak fondness of a doting parent. It is the love of a holy God who, in order to reveal that love and manifest the exceeding glory of that attribute when exercised towards the unworthy, did what was necessary to render its exercise consistent with the other perfections of the divine nature. It was indispensable that God should be just in justifying the ungodly, but he does not thereby cease to be gracious, inasmuch as it was he who provided the ransom by which the objects of his love are redeemed from the curse of the law and the power of sin.

"God cannot declare the unjust to be just"

Another standing objection to the Protestant doctrine has been so often met that nothing but its constant repetition justifies a repetition of the answer. It is said to be absurd that one man should be righteous with the righteousness of another–that for God to pronounce the unjust just is a contradiction. This is a mere play on words. It is, however, very serious play; for it is caricaturing truth. It is indeed certain that the subjective, inherent quality of one person or thing cannot by imputation become the inherent characteristic of any other person or thing. Wax cannot become hard by the imputation of the hardness of a stone; nor can a brute become rational by the imputation of the intelligence of a man; nor the wicked become good by the imputation of the goodness of other men. But what has this to do with one man's assuming the responsibility of another man? If among men the bankrupt can become solvent by a rich man's assuming his responsibilities, then in the court of God may not the guilty become righteous by the Son of God's assuming their responsibilities? If he was made sin for us, why may we not be made the righteousness of God in him? The objection assumes that the word *just* or *righteous* in this connection expresses moral character; whereas in the Bible, when used in relation to this subject, it is always used in a judicial sense, *i.e.,* it expresses the relation of the person spoken of to justice. Δίκαιος is antithetical to ὑπόδικος. The man with regard to whom justice is unsatisfied is ὑπόδικος, "guilty." He with regard to whom justice is satisfied is δίκαιος, "righteous." To declare righteous, therefore, is to declare holy; and to impute righteousness is not to impute goodness, but simply to regard and pronounce those who receive the gift of Christ's righteousness free from condemnation and entitled to eternal life for his sake. Some philosophical theologians seem to think that there is real antagonism between love and justice in the divine nature, or that these attributes are incompatible or inharmonious. This is not so in man; why then should it be so in God? The highest form of moral excellence includes these attributes as essential elements of its perfection. The Scriptures represent them as mysteriously blended in the salvation of man. The Gospel is a revelation to principalities and powers in Heaven of the πολυποίκιλος σοφία τοῦ Θεοῦ, because therein he shows that he can be just and yet justify, love, sanctify, and glorify the chief of sinners; for which all sinners should render him everlasting thanksgiving and praise.

13

Departures from the Protestant Doctrine

Arminian Doctrine

Jacobus Arminius, a man of learning, talents, attractive accomplishments, and exemplary character, was born in Holland in 1560 and died professor in the University of Leyden in 1609, having filled the chair of theology since 1603. His departures from the Reformed doctrines in which he had been educated were far less serious than those of his successors, although involving them, apparently, by a logical necessity. His great difficulty was with the doctrine of predestination or the sovereignty of God in election. He could not, however, get rid of that doctrine without denying the entire inability of man to do what is spiritually good. He, therefore, taught that although mankind fell in Adam and are born in a state of sin and condemnation, and are of themselves entirely unable to turn from sin to holiness, yet they are able to coöperate with the grace of the Holy Spirit given to all men—especially to all who hear the Gospel—in sufficient measure to enable them to repent and believe and to persevere in holy living unto the end. But whether any man does thus repent and believe, or, having believed, perseveres in a holy life, depends on himself and not on God. The purpose of election, therefore, is not a purpose to save, and to that end to give faith and repentance to a definite number of individuals, but a purpose to save those who repent, believe, and persevere in faith until the end. The work of Christ has, therefore, an equal reference to all men. He made full satisfaction to God for the sins of all and every man, so that God can now consistently offer salvation to all men on the conditions laid down in the Gospel.

This is a self-consistent scheme. One part implies or necessitates the admission of the others. The above statement includes all the doctrines presented by the followers of Arminius after his death to the authorities in the form of a Remonstrance, as a justification of their views. Hence the Arminians were called Remonstrants. The document just mentioned contains the five points on which its authors and their associates differed from the Reformed faith. The first relates to predestination, which is explained as the purpose

> illos in Christo, propter Christum et per Christum servare, qui Spiritus Sancti gratia, in eundem ejus filium credunt, et in ea, fideique obedientia, per eandem gratiam in finem perseverant: contra vero eos, qui non convertentur et infideles, in peccato et iræ subjectos relinquere, et condemnare, secundum illud Evang. Joann. iii. 36.*

The second relates to the work of Christ, as to which it is said,

> Proinde Jesum Christum mundi servatorem pro omnibus et singulis mortuum esse, atque ita quidem, ut omnibus per mortem Christi reconciliationem et peccatorum remissionem impetravit: ea tamen conditione, ut nemo illa remissione peccatorum re ipsa fruatur, præter hominem fidelem, et hoc quoque secundum Evang. Joann. iii. 16, et 1 Joann. ii. 2.†

---

* "to save in Christ, because of Christ, and through Christ, those men who believe by the grace of the Holy Spirit, in his same Son, and who persevere in those things until the end, because of the obedience of faith, through the same grace; but otherwise to leave behind and to condemn those who are not converted and are faithless, in sin, and subject to wrath, according to the Gospel of John 3:36."

† "Therefore, Jesus Christ, the Savior of the world, died for each and every one, and

The third, concerning the sinner's ability, declares,

> Hominem vero salutarem fidem a se ipso non habere, nec vi liberi sui arbitrii, quandoquidem in statu defectionis et peccati nihil boni, quandoquidem vere bonum est, quale quid est fides salutaris, ex se possit cogitare, vel facere: sed necessarium esse eum a Deo in Christo per Spiritum Sanctum regigni et renovari mente, affectibus, seu voluntate et omnibus facultatibus, ut aliquid boni possit intelligere, cogitare, velle et perficere. Ev. Joann. xv. 5.*

No Augustinian, whether Lutheran or Calvinist, can say more than that, or desire more to be said by others.

The fourth article, concerning grace, however, shows the point of departure:

> Hanc Dei gratiam esse initium, progressum ac perfectionem omnis boni, atque id eo quidem usque ut ipse homo regenitus absque hac præcedentia, seu adventitia excitante, consequente et cooperante gratia, neque boni quid cogitare, velle, aut facere possit, neque etiam ulli malæ tentatione resistere; adeo quidem ut omnia bona opera, quæ excogitare possumus, Dei gratiæ in Christo tribuenda sint; quod vero modum operationis illius gratiæ, illa non irresistibilis; de multis enim dicitur eos Spiritui Sancto resistere, Act. vii. 51 et alibi multis locis.†

---

so indeed, that through Christ's death he has obtained for all men reconciliation and remission of sins: Nevertheless, on this condition, that no one in fact have the benefit of that remission of sins except the faithful man, and this too is according to the Gospel of John 3:16, and 1 John 2:2."

* "But a man does not have true faith from himself alone, nor from the strength of his free decision, because there is nothing good in a state of weakness and sin, because that truly is good, which healing faith can realize and create from itself. But it is necessary for him to be brought forth again in Christ by God through the Holy Spirit and renewed in his mind, his dispositions, or his will and all his faculties, so that he can understand, realize, desire, and accomplish any good. The Gospel of John 15:5."

† "This grace of God is the beginning, the advancement, and the completion of every

It was not to be expected, in a brief exposition of principles designed for the justification of those who hold them, as members of a Reformed or Calvinistic church, that doubtful terms should be explained. It is beyond controversy, however, and, it is believed, is not controverted, that *irresistible* is here used in the sense of certainly efficacious. The Holy Spirit operates on the hearts of all men. Some are thereby renewed and brought to faith and repentance; others are not. This difference, according to the Arminians, is not to be referred to the nature of the influence exerted, but to the fact that some yield to this grace and coöperate with it, while others reject and resist it.

The fifth article refers to the perseverance of the saints and is indefinite. It admits that the Spirit furnishes grace abundantly sufficient to enable the believer to persevere in holiness:

> Sed an illi ipsi negligentia sua initium sui esse in Christo deserere non possint, et præsentem mundum iterum amplecti, a sancta doctrina ipsis semel tradita deficere, conscientiæ naufragium facere, a gratia excidere; penitus ex sacra Scriptura esset expendum, antequam illud cum plena animi tranquillitate et πληροφορία docere possent.*

Of course no man who believed the doctrine could write thus, and this doubtful mode of expression was soon laid aside, and "falling from grace," in the common sense of the phrase, was admitted to be an Arminian doctrine.

It will be observed that the doctrine of justification is not embraced in the five points in the Remonstrance as presented to

---

good man, and indeed so far that man himself having been reborn without this prerequisite, or by some accident, without the subsequent and cooperating grace, can neither realize, desire, nor perform anything good, nor can he resist any evil temptation; so far as all good works which we are able to devise must indeed be attributed to God's grace in Christ; but in fact that is how that grace works: It is not irresistible, for it is said of many men that they resist the Holy Spirit, Acts 7:51 and in many passages elsewhere."

* "But can it really be that those men themselves are not able, because of their own carelessness, to disregard that their beginning is in Christ, and to embrace the world the authorities in Holland and as made the basis of the decisions of the Synod of Dort. The aberration of the Arminians, however, from the faith of the Reformed churches extended to all the doctrines connected with the plan of salvation. Arminius himself, at least, held far higher and more Scriptural views on original sin, inability, and the necessity of supernatural grace than those which have since become so prevalent even among the Reformed or Calvinistic churches themselves. In matters concerning the method of salvation, especially as to the nature of Christ's work and its application to the believer, they at first adhered closely to the language of the Reformed confessions. Thus they did not hesitate to say that Christ made full satisfaction for the sins of men; that he was a ransom, a sacrifice, a propitiation; that he made expiation for sin; that his righteousness or obedience is the ground of our acceptance with God; that the faith which saves is not mere assent to some random truth or pious confidence in God, but specifically faith in Christ as the Savior of men; and that justification is an act of God pronouncing the sinner just, or in which he pardons sin and accepts the sinner as righteous. All this is satisfactory to the ear. Language, however, admits of different interpretations; and it soon became apparent and avowed that the Remonstrants intended something very different from what the Reformed Church meant to express by the same terms.

The Arminians said that Christ's work was a satisfaction to divine justice. But they did not mean by satisfaction either a "solutio," a real value rendered for what was due; nor even an "acceptio," taking one thing for another as an equivalent; but an "acceptilatio," a gracious acceptance as a satisfaction of that which in its own nature was no equivalent, as though God should accept the life of a brute for that of a man, or faith for perfect obedience. Neither did the Remonstrants mean by *justice* the attribute which requires the righteous distribution of rewards and punishments, and which renders it necessary that the penalty of the law should

---

at hand again, to desert that sacred doctrine that was once handed down to them, to suffer a shipwreck of conscience, to be lost from grace? Inwardly a penalty must be paid, according to the holy Scripture, before they can show that with full tranquility and πληροφορία of spirit."

be executed in case of transgression.

With regard to this latter point (the nature of justice) the language of Grotius, and of the great body of the Remonstrant or Arminian theologians, is perfectly explicit. Grotius says:

> Pœnas infligere, aut a pœnis aliquem liberare, quem punire possis, quod justificare vocat Scriptura, non est nisi rectoris, qua talis primo et per se: ut, puta, in familia patris; in republica regis, in universo Dei. ... Unde sequitur, omnino hic Deum considerandum, ut rectorem.*

Again,[†]

> Ratio [cur "rectori relaxare legem talem non liceat, nisi causa aliqua accedat, si non necessaria, certe sufficiens"] ... est, quod actus ferendi aut relaxandi legem non sit actus absoluti dominii, sed actus imperii, qui tendere debeat ad boni ordinis conservationem.**

> Pœna enim omnis propositum habet bonum commune.[††]

> Prudentia quoque hoc nomine rectorem ad pœnam incitat. Augetur præterea causa puniendi, ubi lex aliqua publicata est, quæ pœnam minatur. Nam tunc omissio

---

* "To inflict punishments, or to free someone from punishments whom you are able to punish, which the Scripture calls justification, does not exist except for a ruler, as such at first and by itself: as, say, in a father's family, in a king's state, in God's universe. ... From which it follows, considering God here altogether as a ruler" (*De Satisfactione Christi*, cap. 2; *Works*, London, 1697, Vol. III, p. 306, b [19-24]).

† *Ibid.*, cap. 5; p. 317, b (35-41).

** "The reason [why 'a ruler is not permitted to relax such a law, unless some reason, if not necessary, then at least sufficient, is an additional factor'] ... is, because the act of proposing or relaxing a law is not an act of unconditional power but an act of command, which ought to extend to the preservation of a good arrangement" (*ibid.*, cap. 2; p. 308, b [62, 63]).

†† "For all punishment has the common good as its purpose."

pœnæ ferme aliquid detrahit de legis authoritate apud subditos.*

Here everything is purely governmental. It is not justice, in the proper and ordinary sense of the word, that is satisfied, but God's wise and benevolent regard to the interests of his moral government. This changes everything. If God's justice be not satisfied, guilt is not removed, sin is not expiated, conscience is not appeased—nor can the real authority and honor of the law be upheld.

As to the other point, the nature of the satisfaction rendered: It was not a real equivalent, which by its intrinsic value met the obligations of the sinner, but it was something graciously accepted as such. Although Grotius rejects the use of the word "acceptilatio," and endeavors to show that it does not express his meaning, nevertheless, though he repudiates the word, he retains the idea. He says, "Ea est pretii natura, ut sui valore aut æstimatione alterum moveat ad concedendam rem, aut jus aliquod, puta impunitatem."†

This amounts to the principle of Duns Scotus that a thing avails (is worth) for what God pleases to take it. Although Grotius does not carry out the principle to the length to which the Schoolmen carried it and say that God might have accepted the death of one man as a satisfaction for the sins of the world, or the blood of bulls or of goats as a real expiation, nevertheless he teaches that God graciously accepted "aliquid pro aliquo," the death of Christ for the death for all the world, not because of its being a real equivalent in itself, but because as ruler, having the right to remit sin without any satisfaction, he saw that the interests of his government could thereby be promoted. Still more clearly is this

---

* "Prudence also urges a ruler to punishment for this purpose. Further, the reason for punishing is increased when some law is published that threatens punishment. For then the omission of punishment usually detracts somewhat from the authority of the law among the subjects" (*ibid.*, cap. 5; p. 316, b [9-13]).

† "It is the nature of value that one moves another to concede a matter, or some right, such as impunity, by virtue of one's own valuation or worth" (*De Satisfactione*, cap. 8; *Works*, London, 1679, Vol. III, p. 328, b [12-14]).

idea expressed by Limborch:

> In eo errant quam maxime, quod velint
> redemtionis pretium per omnia equivalens esse debere
> miseriæ illi, e qua redemtio fit: redemtionis pretium
> enim constitui solet pro libera æstimatione illius, qui
> captivum detinet, non autem solvi pro captivi merito.
> ... Ita pretium, quod Christus persolvit, juxta Dei Patris
> æstimationem persolutum est.*

According to Grotius, Christ died as an example, "exemplum pœnæ." The whole efficacy of his work was its moral impression on the universe. It was not an expiation or satisfaction for past sins, but a means of deterring from the commission of sin in the future. This, as Baur[†] and Strauss[**] remark, is the point in which the theory of Grotius and that of Socinus coincide. They both refer the efficacy of Christ's work to the moral impression which it makes on the minds of intelligent creatures. They refer that moral influence, indeed, to different causes, but moral impression is all the efficacy it has. Although the word *satisfaction* is retained by Grotius, the idea attached to it by the Church is rejected.

The leading Remonstrant or Arminian theologians–Episcopius, Curcellæus, and Limborch–differ from Grotius in their mode of presenting this subject. Instead of regarding the work of Christ as an example of punishment designed to deter from the commission of sin, they adhere to the Scriptural mode of regarding him as a ransom and sacrifice. The difference, however, is more in form than in reality. They admit that Christ redeems us by giving him-

---

* "They err in this most of all, that they desire that the price of redemption in all respects ought to be equal to that unhappiness from which redemption is made; for the price of redemption is usually established according to the free assessment of the one who holds the prisoner, not, however, paid off according to the worth of the prisoner. ... Thus the price which Christ has paid was paid according to the assessment of God the Father" (*Theologia Christiana*, III, xxi, 8, Amsterdam, 1715, p. 262, a).

† *Die christliche Lehre von der Versöhnung*, II, i, 4, Tübingen, 1838, p. 429.

** *Dogmatik*, Tübingen and Stuttgart, 1841, Vol. II, p. 315.

self as a ransom for many. But a ransom, as Curcellæus says, is not an equivalent; it is anything the holder of the captive sees fit to accept. It is admitted, also, that Christ gave himself as a sacrifice for our salvation; but a sacrifice is said not to be a satisfaction to justice, but simply the condition on which pardon is granted. Under the Old Testament, God pardoned sin on the occasion of the sacrifice of irrational animals; under the New Testament, on the occasion of the sacrifice of Christ. "Sacrificia," says Limborch, "non sunt solutiones debitorum, neque plenariæ pro peccatis satisfactiones; sed illis peractis conceditur gratuita peccati remissio." "Redemtionis pretium constitui solet pro libera æstimatione illius, qui captivum detinet."* We know, however, from Scripture that a sacrifice was not merely an arbitrarily appointed antecedent of gratuitous forgiveness; it was not simply an acknowledgment of guilt. We know also that the blood of bulls and of goats under the Old Testament could not take away sin; it availed only to the purifying of the flesh or the remission of ceremonial penalties. The only efficacy of the Old Testament sacrifices, so far as sin committed against God is concerned, was sacramental; that is, they signified, sealed, and applied the benefits of the only real and effectual expiation for sin to those who believed. As the victim symbolically bore the penalty due to the offender, so the eternal Son of God really bore our sins, really became a curse for us, and thus made a true and perfect satisfaction to God for our offenses.

As the Arminians denied that Christ's work was a real satisfaction for sin, they of necessity denied any real justification of the sinner. Justification with them is merely pardon. This is asserted by Grotius in the passage above cited; and even the Rev. Richard Watson, whose excellent system of theology, or *Theological Institutes,* is deservedly in high repute among the Wesleyan Methodists, not only over and over defines justification as pardon, but elaborately argues the question. "The first point," he says,

---

* "Sacrifices are not payments of debts, nor full satisfactions for sins; but they permit the finishing spontaneous remission of sin." "The price of redemption is established only by the free estimation of him who holds the captive" (*Theologia Christiana,* III, xxi, 6, 8, *ut supra,* pp. 261, 1, 262).

"which we find established by the language of the New Testament is, that justification, the pardon and remission of sins, the non-imputation of sin, and the imputation of righteousness, are terms and phrases of the same import."* He then goes on to try to establish that position.

If therefore, pardon and justification are distinct things–the one the executive act of a ruler, the other a judicial act; the one setting aside the demands of justice, the other a declaration that justice is satisfied–then those who reduce justification to mere pardon deny the doctrine of justification as understood and professed by the Lutheran and Reformed churches. It of course is not intended that these Remonstrant or Arminian theologians do not hold what they call justification; nor is it denied that they at times, at least, express their doctrine in the very language of the Confessions of the Protestant churches. Thus the Remonstrants say,

> Justificatio est actio Dei, quam Deus pure pute in sua ipsius mente efficit, quia nihil aliud est, quam volitio aut decretum, quo peccata remittere, et justitiam imputare aliquando vult iis, qui credunt, id est, quo vult pœnas, peccatis eorum promeritas, iis non infligere, eosque tanquam justos tractare et premio afficere.†

Nevertheless, they tell us that they mean by this only pardon. Protestants, when they say justification includes pardon "and" the imputation of righteousness, mean two distinct things by pardon and imputation of righteousness. The Remonstrants regard them as identical, and, therefore, can use the very language of Protestants while rejecting their doctrine. As everyone knows that when a criminal is pardoned by the executive and allowed to resume his

---

* II, xxiii; New York, 1832, p. 426.

† "Justification is an act of God, which God at times produces purely in his own mind, because nothing is changed, as to will or decree, because he wishes to remit sin and impute righteousness to him who believes; that is, because he wishes not to inflict the punishment which his sins deserve, and so to influence and treat the righteous" (*Apologia pro Confessione Remonstrantium,* cap. 11, 12; Episcopii *Opera,* Rotterdam, 1665, Vol. II, p. 166, a, of second set).

rights of property and right of voting, he is not thereby justified; so every candid mind must admit that there is an immense difference between the Remonstant or Arminian doctrine of justification and that held as the cardinal principle of the Reformation by both Lutherans and Reformed.

This difference becomes still more apparent when we consider what the Arminians make the ground of justification. As they deny that Christ made any real satisfaction to divine justice (as distinguished from benevolence), so they deny that the righteousness of Christ is imputed to the believer as the ground of his justification. On this point, Limborch says,

> Hæc autem, quæ nobis imputatur, non est Christi justitia; nusquam enim Scriptura docet, Christi justitiam nobis imputari; sed tantum fidem nobis imputari in justitiam, et quidem propter Christum.*

And Curcellæus says,

> Nullibi docet Scriptura justitiam Christi nobis imputari. Et id absurdum est. Nemo enim in se injustus aliena justitia potest esse formaliter justus, no magis, quam aliena albedine Æthiops esse albus.†

As the righteousness of Christ is not imputed to the believer, the ground of his justification—that which is accepted as righteousness—is faith and its fruits, or faith and evangelical obedience. On this subject Limborch says that under the new covenant God demands

> obedientiam fidei, hoc est, non rigidam et omnibus

---

* "That itself, which is imputed to us, is not the righteousness of Christ; indeed Scripture nowhere teaches that the righteousness of Christ is imputed to us, but only faith is imputed to us as righteousness and indeed because of Christ" (*Theologia Christiana,* VI, iv, 18, *ut supra,* p. 703, a).

† "Not one Scripture teaches that the righteousness of Christ is imputed to us. And it is absurd. Indeed no one in himself unrighteous can be formally righteous with the righteousness that belongs to another, any more than an Ethiopian is white because of a whiteness that belongs to another" (*Relig. Christ. Inst.* 7, 9, 6).

æqualem, prout exigebat lex; sed tantam, quantam fides, id est, certa de divinis promissionibus persuasio, in unoquoque efficere potest; in qua etiam Deus multas imperfectiones et lapsus condonat, modo animo sincero præceptorum ipsius observationi incumbamus, et continuo in eadem proficere studeamus.*

And again, "Deus non judicat hominum justitiam esse perfectam, imo eam judicat esse imperfectam; sed justitiam, quam imperfectam judicat, gratiose accipit ac si perfecta esset."[†]

He, therefore, thus defines justification,

Est gratiosa æstimatio, seu potius acceptatio justitiæ nostræ imperfectæ (quæ, si Deus rigide nobiscum agere vellet, in judicio Dei nequaquam consistere posset) pro perfecta, propter Jesus Christum.**

The same view is presented when he speaks of faith in its relation to justification. Faith is said to be imputed for righteousness; but Limborch says, "Sciendum, quando dicimus, nos fide justificari, nos non excludere opera, quæ fides exigit et tanquam fœcunda mater producit; sed ea includere."[††]

---

* "the obedience of faith, that is, not rigid and equal obedience from all, just as the law demands; but only as much as faith, that is, a certain conviction about divine promises, can produce in each man. In that God also overlooks our imperfections and faults, only with a sincere spirit may we concentrate on the observation of his commands and immediately be eager to make progress in those same commands" (*Theologia Christiana*, VI, iv, 37, *ut supra*, p. 706, a).

† "God does not judge that the righteousness of men is perfect; no, he judges that it is imperfect, but he freely accepts that righteousness, which he judges imperfect, as if it were perfect" (*ibid.*, VI, iv, 41; p. 706, b, 707, a).

** "It is a favorable valuation, or rather acceptance of our imperfect righteousness (which, if God wished to act inflexibly with us, could by no means stand in God's judgment) as perfect, because of Jesus Christ" (*ibid.*, VI, iv, 18; p. 703, 1).

†† "It must be known that when we say that we are justified by means of faith, we do not exclude works that faith demands just as a fruitful mother brings forth; but we include them" (*ibid.*, VI, iv, 32; p. 705, b).

Again,

> Fides est conditio in nobis et a nobis requisita, ut justificationem consequamur. Est itaque talis actus, qui, licet in se spectatus perfectus nequaquam sit, sed in multis deficiens, tamen a Deo gratiosa et liberrima voluntate pro pleno et perfecto acceptatur et propter quem Deus homini gratiose remissionem peccatorum et vitæ æternæ præmium conferre vult.*

Fletcher says:

> With respect to the Christless law of paradisaical obedience, we entirely disclaim sinless perfection.
>
> We shall not be judged by that law, but by a law adapted to our present state and circumstances, a milder law, called the law of Christ.
>
> Our Heavenly Father never expects of us, in our debilitated state, the obedience of immortal Adam in paradise.†

Dr. Peck says, "The standard of character set up in the Gospel must be such as is practicable by man, fallen as he is. Coming up to this standard is what we call Christian perfection."**

Under the covenant of works as made with Adam, perfect obedience was the condition of acceptance with God and of eternal life; under the Gospel, for Christ's sake, imperfect, or evangelical obedience, is the ground of justification, *i.e.,* it is that

---

* "Faith is a condition in us and required of us, so that we may obtain justification. And so it is such an act, which although having been seen is by no means perfect in itself, but failing in many things, nevertheless is accepted as full and complete by God, because of his favorable and very unrestrained will, and because of which God graciously wishes to attribute to man remission of sins and the reward of eternal life" (*ibid.*, VI, iv, 31; p. 705, a).

† *Last Check to Antinomianism*, sect. i; *Works*, New York, 1833, Vol. II, pp. 493-494.

** *Christian Perfection*, New York, 1843, p. 294.

(propter quam) on account of which God graciously grants us the remission of sin and the reward of eternal life.

Summary

We have then the three great systems. First, that of the Romanists which teaches that on account of the work of Christ God grants, through Christian baptism, an infusion of divine grace by which all sin is purged from the soul and all ground for the infliction of the penalty is removed and the sinner rendered inherently just or holy. This is the first justification. Then in virtue of the new principle of spiritual life thus imparted, the baptized or regenerated are enabled to perform good works, which are really meritorious and on account of which they are admitted to Heaven.

Second, the Arminian theory, that on account of what Christ has done, God is pleased to grant sufficient grace to all men and to accept the imperfect obedience which the believer is thus enabled to render in lieu of the perfect obedience required under the covenant made with Adam; and on account of that imperfect obedience, eternal life is graciously bestowed.

Third, the Protestant doctrine that Christ, as the representative and substitute of sinners or of his people, takes their place under the law; and in their name and in their behalf fulfils all righteousness, thereby making a real, perfect, and infinitely meritorious satisfaction to the law and justice of God. This righteousness is imputed, or set to the account of the believer, who is thereupon and on that account freely pardoned and pronounced righteous in the sight of God and entitled not only to the remission of sin but also to eternal life. Being united to Christ by faith, the believer becomes partaker of his life, so that it is not he that lives but Christ that lives in him; and the life which the believer now lives in the flesh is by faith in the Son of God who loved him and gave himself for him.

Comparison of the Different Doctrines

The first remark which suggests itself on the comparison of these several schemes is that the relation between the believer and Christ is far more close, peculiar, and constant on the Protestant scheme than on any other. He is dependent on him every hour–for the imputation of his righteousness, for the supplies of the Spirit of life, and for his care, guidance, and intercession. He must look to him continually, and continually exercise faith in him as an ever-present Savior in order to live. According to the other schemes, Christ has merely made the salvation of all men possible. There his work ended. According to Romanists, he has made it possible that God should give sanctifying grace in baptism; according to the Arminians, he has rendered it possible for him to give sufficient grace to all men whereby to sanctify and save themselves. We are well aware that this is theory; that the true people of God, whether Romanists or Remonstrants, do not look on Christ thus as a Savior afar off. They doubtless have the same exercises toward him that their fellow believers have; nevertheless, such is the doctrine. The doctrine places a great gulf between the soul and Christ.

Second, it hardly admits of question that the Protestant view conforms to the Scriptural mode of presenting the plan of salvation. Christ in the Bible is declared to be the head of his people, their representative; they were in him in such a sense that they died in him; they are raised with him and sit with him in heavenly places. They were in him as the race was in Adam, and as branches are in the vine. They individually receive the sprinkling of that blood which cleanses from all sin. They are constituted righteous by his obedience. As he was made sin for them, so are they made the righteousness of God in him. He is not only an example of punishment as Grotius represents, a mere governmental device, but a sacrifice substituted for us on whose head every believer must lay his hand and to whom he must transfer the burden of his sins.

Third, what is included indeed in the above, but is so important and decisive as to require distinct and repeated mention: All schemes, other than the Protestant, refer the proximate ground of our acceptance with God to our own subjective character. It is because of our own goodness that we are regarded and treated as righteous. Concsience demands, the Scriptures reveal, and the believer instinctively seeks something better than that. His own goodness is badness. It cannot satisfy his own bleared vision; how then can it appear before the eyes of God? It matters not how the Romanist may exalt his "inward habits of grace" or how the Arminian may sublimate his evangelical obedience to perfection; neither can satisfy either the conscience or God.

Fourth, the Protestant doctrine is the only one on which the devout soul can live. This has been urged before when speaking of the work of Christ. It is fair to appeal from theology to hymnology. It is enough to say on this point that Lutheran and Reformed Christians can find nowhere, out of the Bible, more clear, definite, soul-satisfying expression of their doctrinal views upon this subject than are to be found in many of the hymns of the Latin and Arminian churches. As a single example may be cited the following stanzas from John Wesley's "Hymns and Spiritual Songs":

> Join, Earth and Heaven to bless
> The Lord our Righteousness.
> The mystery of redemption this,
> This the Savior's strange design—
> Man's offence was counted his,
> Ours his righteousness divine.
>
> In him complete we shine;
> His death, his life, is mine;
> Fully am I justified;
> Free from sin, and more than free,
> Guiltless, since for me he died;
> Righteous, since he lived for me.

Scripture Index

Acts

7:51	*130n.*
13:39	*28*
15:1, 24	*67*
20:28	*80*

Colossians

1:20	*23*
1:21, 22	*24*
1:27	*55*
2:10	*56*
2:14	*24, 54*

1 Corinthians

1:23, 24	*15*
1:27-31	*31*
1:30	*15, 28, 55, 99*
2:8	*80*
6:11	*28*
12:12, 27	*55*
15:20	*22*
15:22	*22, 55*

2 Corinthians

5:14	*22*
5:19	*81, 109*
5:20	*16*
5:21	*16, 28, 100*

Deuteronomy

24:13	*116*
25:1	*3, 47*

Ephesians

1:4	*55*
1:6	*104*
1:7	*23*
1:23	*55*
2:1-6	*55*
2:4-6	*22*
2:8	*31*
2:9	*10, 31*
2:10	*10*
2:13	*23*
2:15	*24*
2:16	*24*
3:19	*56*
4:16	*55*

Exodus

23:7	*3, 47*

Ezekiel

17:20	*17*

Galatians

1:4	*24*
2:16	*47, 72*
2:19	*12, 54*
2:20	*22, 55*
2:21	*4*
3:1-2	*13*
3:6	*115*
3:10	*4, 5, 72*
3:11, 12	*8*

3:13   *16, 99*
3:14   *94*
3:16   *116*
3:24, 25   *12*
3:26   *57*
3:36   *109*
4:4, 5   *15, 79, 99*
4:21-31   *13*
5:1-4   *13*
5:3   *4*
5:4   *47*

Genesis
15   *115*

Hebrews
5:1   *25*
7:12, 18, 19   *26*
7:16   *25*
7:25   *25*
7:28   *25*
9:12   *26*
9:13   *20*
9:14   *20, 25, 26*
9:18   *19*
9:24   *26*
9:25   *26*
9:26   *26*
9:28   *17, 26*
10:5-15   *21*
12:22, 24   *23*

Isaiah
5:23   *3, 47*
53:6, 11, 12   *17*

James
2   *73*

Jeremiah
23:6   *15*

Job
9:20   *49*
32:2   *48*
34:17   *49*

John
1:29   *20*
3:16   *30, 129*
3:17   *50*
3:18   *35, 50*
3:36   *128*
15:1-12   *55*
15:4   *35*
15:5   *35, 129*
17:9   *122*

1 John
1:7   *23, 56, 102*
2:2   *20, 129*
3:5   *17*
4:9, 10   *30*

Lamentations
5:7   *17*

Leviticus
1:4   *18*
7:18   *81*
8:14   *18*
16:21, 22   *18*
17:4   *81*
20:17   *16*
24:15   *16*

Luke
7:29   *48*

10:28	2
10:29	47
16:15	47
22:20	23

Matthew
11:19	47
19:17	2
20:28	24, 101
26:28	23
27:24	46

Numbers
| 9:13 | 17 |
| 14:33 | 17 |

1 Peter
1:2	23
1:18, 19	20
2:24	17, 54
3:18	24

Philippians
2:6-8	80
3:4-9	28
3:8-9	99
3:9	15, 72, 93

Proverbs
| 17:15 | 47 |

Psalms
32:2	81
51:4	48
106:31	116
110:4	25
143:2	7

Revelation
1:5	23
5:9	23
22:11	3n., 48

Romans
1:18	51
2:2	77
2:13	3, 46
2:14	71
2:26	115
2:31	14
3:10-12	7
3:19	51, 71
3:20	3, 72
3:21	94
3:23	5
3:24	28
3:25	20, 98
3:29	32
3:31	34
4:1-3	92
4:3	9, 94, 115
4:4	72
4:5	47, 117
4:6	49, 81, 92
4:6-8	98
4:7-8	7, 50
4:9	94
4:22	115
4:24	92, 94
4:25	24
5:1	39, 56
5:6	24
5:8	30
5:9	23, 28, 93, 95, 98

5:10	*24, 57, 95*	9:30-32	*27*
5:12-21	*55, 58, 79*	10:3	*27, 72, 93, 98*
5:16	*96*	10:4	*98*
5:17	*28, 92*	10:5	*2, 5*
5:18	*50, 93, 96*	10:9	*94*
5:19	*15, 28, 46, 73,*	10:12, 13	*32*
	79, 92, 93, 96	11:6	*31*
6:1-8	*55*		
6:5	*22*	**1 Samuel**	
6:7	*22*	22:15	*81*
6:8	*22*		
6:14	*12, 54, 108*	**2 Samuel**	
6:15	*14*	19:19	*81*
6:23	*2*		
7:1-6	*12*	**1 Timothy**	
7:4	*22, 54, 79*	2:5-6	*101*
7:7	*72*		
7:12	*72*	**2 Timothy**	
7:24	*61*	1:9	*10*
8:1	*28, 49*		
8:3	*57*	**Titus**	
8:6	*54*	3:5	*10, 72*
8:17	*58, 109*		
8:32	*24*	**Zechariah**	
8:33, 34	*3*	6:13	*25*

INDEX

Aaron, 18

Abraham, 8-9, 94, 111, 115, 117

Adam, 15, 22, 50, 58, 70, 75, 79, 95-96, 101, 114, 127, 139-141

adoption, 106, 109

angels, 13, 25, 104

Anselm, 96

Apologia pro Confessione Remonstrantium, 136n.

Apology for the Augsburg Confession, 38n., 39n.

apostasy, 13

Arminianism, 70, 75, 114, 128, 130-131, 142

Arminius, Jacobus, 127

Articles of Religion, 87

assent, 111

atonement, 18, 21, 23, 53

attainder, 78

Augsburg Confession, 38n.

baptism, 70, 96, 107, 111-112, 140-141

Baur, Bruno, 130; *Works: Die christliche Lehre von der Versöhnung*, 134n.

belief, 49; *see also* faith

Bellarmin, Robert, 59-60, 73, 74n., 77, 81, 83, 106-107, 113-114; *Works: De Amissione Gratia et Statu Peccati*, 107n.; *De Justificatione*, 73n., 84n., 107n., 114n.

benevolence, 50, 54

Bernard, 69n.

blood, 20, 23, 81

Books of Homilies, 87

Calvin, John, 61-65; *Works: Institutio*, 61n., 62n., 66n., 83n.

Calvinism, 129

ceremonies, 67

character, 92

charity, 63, 74, 113

Christ, Jesus, 4, 13-14, 16-17, 20-22, 25-27, 29-30, 32, 34-36, 38, 41, 46, 49, 57-58, 61, 66, 68, 71-73, 78, 81, 89, 92-94, 97-101, 104, 110-113, 116, 118, 121, 123, 128-129, 131, 1 3 3 -137, 140-141; active and passive obedience of, 89; blood of, 73; death of, 22-24, 63, 96, 102; God's grace in, 130; merit of, 62, 70, 107; obedience of, 105, 119; propitiation of, 109; righteousness of, 42, 63, 79-81, 84, 86-87, 95, 97-98, 108, 120,

122, 137; union with, 23, 55, 63, 75, 140; *see also* God

Christian Perfection (Peck), 139n.

Christliche Lehre von der Versöhnung, Die (Baur), 134n.

church, 80, 92, 96, 120

Church of England, 86

clergy, 97

condemnation, 27, 35, 42, 48-49, 58, 60, 63, 85-86, 95-96, 110, 126-127

conduct, 92

confession, 6, 19, 61

confessions, 82, 131

confidence, 117, 131

conscience, 6, 32, 36, 54, 56, 59-60, 77, 103, 107, 118, 130, 133, 142

conversion, 64

covenant, 70, 98, 109

covetousness, 10

creation, 30

crime, 123

cross, of Jesus, 23-24

Curcellaeus, 77, 134, 137; *Works: Relig. Christ. Instit.*, 137n.

curse, 4, 14-17, 21, 75, 79, 92-93, 99, 101, 122, 124-125, 135

David, 7, 97

De Amissione Gratia et Statu Peccati (Bellarmin), 107n.

De Justificatione (Bellarmin), 73n., 84n., 107n., 114n.

De Satisfactione Christi (Grotius), 132n., 133n.

De Wette, 48, 99

death, 2, 12, 15-16, 19, 22-24, 27, 51, 53, 55, 57, 75, 97, 102, 119

Decalogue, 71

deeds, 68

demons, 74

Devil, 121

Doctrina Christianae Religionis (Vitringa), 86n.

Dogmatik (Strauss), 68, 134

Dogmatik der evangelisch-lutherischen Kirche, dargestellt und aus den Quellen belegt, Die (Schmid), 82n.

Ebrard, J.H.A., 46; *Works: Christliche Dogmatik,* 46n.

Edwards, Jonathan, 41-42, 87-88; *Works: Works of President Edwards,* 42n., 87n.

elect, 23, 49, 61, 80

election, 127

Episcopius, 134

equivocation, 69n.

evil, 35, 102

expiation, 53, 77, 90, 102, 107, 110, 131, 133-135

faith, 4, 13-14, 20, 28, 32, 35-37, 41-43, 57, 63, 65-67, 75, 90-93, 99, 103, 110-111, 114-115, 117-119, 122-123, 127-131, 137-139, 141; Abraham's, 116

fall, 67, 70, 94

Fenelon, 69n.

Fletcher, 139; *Works: Last Check to Antinomianism,* 139n.

forgiveness, 18, 60, 97

Form of Concord, 38n., 40, 90, 105

Gentiles, 5, 10, 13-14, 27, 31, 51, 72, 74, 93-94

Glaubenslehre der evangelisch-reformirten Kirche, dargestellt und aus den Quellen belegt, Die (Schweizer), 82n.

goats, 18, 20, 26

God, 1, 3, 9, 16, 21, 26, 28, 30-34, 38, 40, 42, 47, 57-58, 61, 67-68, 71, 74, 76-78, 81, 83, 91-95, 97, 99, 101, 110-116, 121, 125, 129, 132-133, 138-139; confidence in, 111; curse of, 109; the Father, 83, 85-86, 90, 100, 113, 122, 124, 134, 139; glory of, 30; justice of, 63; Lamb of, 124; law of, 2, 41, 76, 110; love of, 29-31; power of, 35; righteousness of, 52, 72, 91, 97, 113; the Son, 15, 60, 86, 95, 100, 102, 104; sovereignty of, 127; the Holy Spirit, 13, 21, 25, 63, 70, 101-102, 107, 112-113, 121-122, 127-130; wrath of, 24; *see also* Christ

Gospel, 16, 20, 24, 31, 35, 52, 70, 72, 82, 87, 92-93, 103-104, 109-110, 115, 118, 123-124, 127-129, 139

grace, 7, 12-13, 30-31, 36-37, 42, 47, 64, 70, 72-73, 84, 86, 120, 122-124, 127, 129, 131, 140, 142; falling from, 130; ha-

bitual, 61; irresistible, 130; subjective, 106

Greeks, 15, 24

Grotius, Hugo, 132-135, 141; *Works: De Satisfactione Christi*, 132n., 133n.

guilt, 32, 40, 47, 56, 58-60, 64, 87, 102, 107, 110, 121, 123, 133, 135

Hase, 40n.; *Works: Libri Symbolici*, 40n., 90n.

heart, 14; written upon, 2

heathen, 2

Heaven, 1, 26, 51, 58, 93, 101, 103, 110, 115-116, 126, 140

Hebrews, 19-20, 25

Heidelberg Catechism, 36

heirs, 58

Hell, 80

History of Christian Doctrine (Shedd), 89n.

holiness, 14, 29, 35, 58, 61, 106, 122, 127

Holy Ghost, *see* God

hope, 61

Hutterus Redivivius, 40n.

hymnology, 142

imputation, 3, 41-42, 63, 66, 75, 81, 87, 91, 95-98, 105, 109-110, 116, 120, 122, 125, 137-138, 141

inability, 131

influence, moral, 134

infusion, 45, 52-54, 56, 58-59, 62-65, 70, 73-74, 81, 84, 102,

105-107, 111-112, 140
Institutio (Calvin), 61n., 62n., 66n., 83n.
Institutiones Theologiae (Wegscheider), 68n.
intercession, 26, 110, 141
Isaiah, 19

James, 73
Jesus, *see* Christ
Jews, 5, 10, 15, 19, 24, 27-28, 31, 51, 72, 74, 93-95, 98
John, 80
Judaism, 13, 120
judgment,1-3, 48, 50, 63
justice, 16, 29-30, 33, 42, 47, 50-51, 54, 56, 64, 73, 78, 108-110, 122-123, 126, 131, 133-134, 136-137, 140
justification, *passim*; first, 74, 111-112, 114, 140; second, 61, 74, 111, 114; subjective, 45, 49, 58, 60, 102-104

Kant, Immanuel, 68
knowledge, 63

language, 2, 108
Last Check to Antinomianism (Fletcher), 139
law, 4-6, 10, 14, 11-18, 26-28, 33, 35, 47, 50-51, 56-57, 63, 67, 71-72, 75, 78-79, 83, 88-90, 94, 98-101, 108, 118, 123-125, 133, 140; ceremonial, 10, 14; immutability of, 63; Mosaic, 101; obedience to, 43; penalty of, 43

Lazarus, 122
liberty, 13, 15
Libri Symbolici (Streitwolf), 113n.
license, 120
licentiousness, 14
life, eternal, 22, 41, 56-57, 60-63, 69n., 78, 82, 92, 100, 102, 105, 110, 112-114, 118, 126, 139-140
Limborch, 70-71, 133-135, 137-138; Works: *Theologia Christiana*, 71n.
Logos, 80
Lombard, Peter, 62
love, 34
Luther, Martin, 40, 62
Lutheranism, 71, 105, 129, 136

Melchizedek, 25
mercy, 10, 33, 37, 63, 110-111
merit, 83, 112, 114; condign, 70, 112; congruent, 112
Messiah, 8, 17, 19, 24, 94, 123
Methodists, Weslyan, 135
mind, state of, 104, 117
modernism, 69n.
Moehler, 77; *Works: Symbolik*, 77n. ᾽
morality, 121
Moses, 10, 13, 67, 71, 118

nature, law of, 71
Niemeyer, 38; *Works: Collectio Confessionum*, 38

obedience, 2-5, 8-10, 14-15, 23, 27, 29, 34, 41, 51, 57, 61, 70-

71, 73, 83, 87-88, 92-95, 96, 115, 118, 131, 138-140; active, 79; Christ's, 89; evangelical, 71, 75, 137, 139, 142; passive, 79; perfect, 88, 131
Onesimus, 81
Opera Episcopii, 136
Owen, John, 84, 86-87; *Works: Justification*, 86n., 87n., 97n.

pardon, 19, 23, 29, 33, 35-36, 45, 48-49, 51, 53, 56-57, 63-65, 78, 95, 99-101, 103, 107-108, 121, 134-136, 140
Paul, 4, 13, 16, 22, 27-28, 47, 49, 52, 60-61, 72, 74-75, 80-82, 93, 94, 97-99, 101, 116, 121-122
peace, 29, 33-35, 56, 58-60, 63, 95, 99
Peck, 139; *Works: Christian Perfection*, 139n.
Pelagianism, 67, 75, 111
penalty, 14-16, 41, 49-50, 52-53, 79, 88-89, 107-108, 130, 135, 140
penance, 51
perfection, 139
perseverance, 127, 130
Philemon, 81
Phinehas, 81, 116
Pilate, Pontius, 46
pollution, 32
power, 92-93, 121
preaching, 24
predestination, 127-128
priest, 25-26
promise, 94, 116

property, 136
prophets, 101
propitiation, 8, 17-18, 20, 23, 30, 34, 94, 98, 102, 117, 131
punishment, 17-19, 21, 37, 40, 60, 107

Quenstedt, 41n.

ransom, 53, 73, 101, 117, 119, 125, 131, 134
rationalists, 67, 75, 111
reason, 32, 91, 96, 103, 121
reconciliation, 18-19, 21, 24, 56-57, 60, 92, 95, 101, 122
redemption, 15, 20, 30-31, 35; covenant of, 100
Reformation, 48, 52, 61, 82, 88, 92, 107, 136
Reformers, 45, 63, 136
regeneration, 43, 52, 61, 69n., 70, 71, 75, 107, 111-112
Relig. Christ. Inst. (Curcellaeus), 137n.
religious teachers, 1
remission, 23, 63, 66, 106-107, 129, 135, 139-140
Remonstrants, 70, 115, 128, 130-131, 136
repentance, 6, 50, 58, 127, 130
restoration, 45, 53
Resurrection, 22, 69n., 90
revelation, 10, 94, 101, 126
reward, 40, 43, 57, 78
righteousness, 3, 15, 27-29, 33, 36-38, 40-41, 46-47, 49, 55-56, 58, 63-64, 66, 70, 73-74, 78,

90-91, 105, 107, 121, 125; active, 89; Christ's, 63, 83, 88, 96, 126; imputation of, 121; infusion of, 107; inherent, 8, 84, 112; passive, 89; subjective, 63
rites, 9, 67
Roman Catholicism, 45, 58, 61, 63, 70, 76, 77, 103, 105, 107, 111-112, 114, 116, 140-142
rulers, 29

sacraments, 74
sacrifice, 17, 19-21
salvation, 23, 29, 35, 50, 52
sanctification, 12, 42, 45, 48-49, 52, 63, 69n., 75, 95, 100, 102, 105, 107, 113, 117, 120, 122, 126, 141
satisfaction, 41, 53, 56, 64, 88-89, 128, 131, 133, 134-135, 137, 140
Schmid, 82; *Works: Die Dogmatik der evangelisch-lutherischen Kirche, dargestellt und aus den Quellen belegt*, 82n.
Schweizer, 82; *Works: Die Glaubenslehre der evangelisch-reformirten Kirche, dargestellt und aus den Quellen belegt*, 82n.
Scotus, Duns, 133
Scripture, analogy of, 115
Second Helvetic Confession, 37
Shedd, W.G.T., 88-89; *Works: History of Christian Doctrine*, 89n.
Shiloh, 116
sin, 2, 7-8, 14-17, 19-21, 24-25,

27, 30, 33-36, 40, 46, 49, 51, 53, 56, 58, 60, 64-65, 70, 74, 78, 82-83, 90, 94, 97-100, 107-109, 117, 120-121, 124-125, 127-129, 131, 133-134, 140-141; Adam's, 96; forgiveness of, 37; original, 131; pardon of, 105; pollution of, 105; remission of, 105, 107
slaves, 13
Socinus, 140
Solida Declaratio, 61
Steudlin, 68
Strauss, David, 68, 134; *Works: Dogmatik*, 68n.
Streitwolf, 106n., 113n.
substitution, 18-19, 21, 100, 102, 123-124
Symbolik, 77n.
Synod of Dort, 131

theocracy, 18
Theologiae Christiana (Limborch), 71, 134, 137n., 138n., 139n.
Theological Institutes, 135n.
theology, 142
Thomas, 80
Tischendorf, 48
tradition, 20
Trent, Council of, 74, 112, 117
Trinity, 69n.
trust, 117
truth, 13, 29, 33, 68
Turretin, Francis, 82-84; *Works: Institutio*, 83n., 84n.

Vitringa, Campegius, 85; *Works: Doctrina Christianae Religionis,* 86n.

Watson, Richard, 135
Wegscheider, 68; *Works: Institutiones Theologiae,* 68n.
Wesley, John, 142
Westminster Catechism, 36
wisdom, 29, 35, 47, 54, 76, 91, 99, 117

works, 4-9, 13, 16, 26, 28, 31, 34, 47, 49, 65, 68-75, 81, 92, 98, 104, 112, 114, 117-118, 120, 123, 129, 132-133, 138-140; ceremonial, 71; covenant of, 110, 139; good, 61; ritual,75 wrath of God, 83, 85, 93, 108, 128

Zechariah, 25

THE CRISIS OF OUR TIME

Historians have christened the thirteenth century the Age of Faith and termed the eighteenth century the Age of Reason. The twentieth century has been called many things: the Atomic Age, the Age of Inflation, the Age of the Tyrant, the Age of Aquarius. But it deserves one name more than the others: the Age of Irrationalism. Contemporary secular intellectuals are anti-intellectual. Contemporary philosophers are anti-philosophy. Contemporary theologians are anti-theology.

In past centuries, secular philosophers have generally believed that knowledge is possible to man. Consequently they expended a great deal of thought and effort trying to justify knowledge. In the twentieth century, however, the optimism of the secular philosophers has all but disappeared. They despair of knowledge.

Like their secular counterparts, the great theologians and doctors of the church taught that knowledge is possible to man. Yet the theologians of the twentieth century have repudiated that belief. They also despair of knowledge. This radical skepticism has filtered down from the philosophers and theologians and penetrated our entire culture, from television to music to literature. *The Christian in the twentieth century is confronted with an overwhelming cultural consensus—sometimes stated explicitly but most often implicitly: Man does not and cannot know anything truly.*

What does this have to do with Christianity? Simply this: If man can know nothing truly, man can truly know nothing. We cannot know that the Bible is the Word of God, that Christ died for his people, or that Christ is alive today at the right hand of the Father. Unless knowledge is possible, Christianity is nonsensical, for it claims to be knowledge. What is at stake in the twentieth century is not simply a single doctrine, such as the Virgin Birth, or the existence of Hell, as important as those doctrines may be, but the whole of Christianity itself. If knowledge is not possible to man, it is worse than silly to argue points of doctrine–it is insane.

The irrationalism of the present age is so thoroughgoing and pervasive that even the Remnant–the segment of the professing church that remains faithful–has accepted much of it, frequently without even being aware of what it was accepting. In some circles this irrationalism has become synonymous with piety and humility, and those who oppose it are denounced as rationalists–as though to be logical were a sin. Our contemporary anti-theologians make a contradiction and call it a Mystery. The faithful ask for truth and are given Paradox. If any balk at swallowing the absurdities of the anti-theologians, they are frequently marked as heretics or schismatics who seek to act independently of God.

There is no greater threat facing the true Church of Christ at this moment than the irrationalism that now controls our entire culture. Totalitarianism, guilty of tens of millions of murders–including those of millions of Christians–is to be feared, but not nearly so much as the idea that we do not and cannot know the truth. Hedonism, the popular philosophy of America, is not to be feared so much as the belief that logic–that "mere human logic," to use the religious irrationalists' own phrase–is futile. The attacks on truth, on revelation, on the intellect, and on logic are renewed daily. But note well: The misologists–the haters of logic– use logic to demonstrate the futility of using logic. The anti-intellectuals construct intricate intellectual arguments to prove the insufficiency of the intellect. The anti-theologians use the revealed Word of God to show that there can be no revealed Word of God– or that if there could, it would remain impenetrable darkness and Mystery to our finite minds.

Nonsense Has Come

Is it any wonder that the world is grasping at straws—the straws of experientialism, mysticism, and drugs? After all, if people are told that the Bible contains insoluble mysteries, then is not a flight into mysticism to be expected? On what grounds can it be condemned? Certainly not on logical grounds or Biblical grounds, if logic is futile and the Bible unintelligible. Moreover, if it cannot be condemned on logical or Biblical grounds, it cannot be condemned at all. If people are going to have a religion of the mysterious, they will not adopt Christianity: They will have a genuine mystery religion. "Those who call for Nonsense," C.S. Lewis once wrote, "will find that it comes." And that is precisely what has happened. The popularity of Eastern mysticism, of drugs, and of religious experience is the logical consequence of the irrationalism of the twentieth century. There can and will be no Christian reformation—and no reconstruction of society—unless and until the irrationalism of the age is totally repudiated by Christians.

The Church Defenseless

Yet how shall they do it? The spokesmen for Christianity have been fatally infected with irrationalism. The seminaries, which annually train thousands of men to teach millions of Christians, are the finishing schools of irrationalism, completing the job begun by the government schools and colleges. Some of the pulpits of the most conservative churches (we are not speaking of the apostate churches) are occupied by graduates of the anti-theological schools. These products of modern anti-theological education, when asked to give a reason for the hope that is in them, can generally respond with only the intellectual analogue of a shrug—a mumble about Mystery. They have not grasped—and therefore cannot teach those for whom they are responsible—the first truth: "And you shall know the truth." Many, in fact, explicitly deny it, saying that, at best, we possess only "pointers" to the truth, or something "similar" to the truth, a mere analogy. Is the impotence of the Christian church a puzzle? Is the fascination with pentecostalism and faith healing among members of conser-vative churches an enigma? Not when one understands the sort of studied nonsense that is purveyed in the name of God in the seminaries.

The Trinity Foundation

The creators of The Trinity Foundation firmly believe that theology is too important to be left to the licensed theologians – the graduates of the schools of theology. They have created The Trinity Foundation for the express purpose of teaching the faithful all that the Scriptures contain–not warmed over, baptized, secular philosophies. Each member of the board of directors of The Trinity Foundation has signed this oath: "I believe that the Bible alone and the Bible in its entirety is the Word of God and, therefore, inerrant in the autographs. I believe that the system of truth presented in the Bible is best summarized in the Westminster Confession of Faith. So help me God."

The ministry of The Trinity Foundation is the presentation of the system of truth taught in Scripture as clearly and as completely as possible. We do not regard obscurity as a virtue, nor confusion as a sign of spirituality. Confusion, like all error, is sin, and teaching that confusion is all that Christians can hope for is doubly sin.

The presentation of the truth of Scripture necessarily involves the rejection of error. The Foundation has exposed and will continue to expose the irrationalism of the twentieth century, whether its current spokesman be an existentialist philosopher or a professed Reformed theologian. We oppose anti-intellectualism, whether it be espoused by a neo-orthodox theologian or a fundamentalist evangelist. We reject misology, whether it be on the lips of a neo-evangelical or those of a Roman Catholic charismatic.

To each error we bring the brilliant light of Scripture, proving all things, and holding fast to that which is true.

The Primacy of Theory

The ministry of The Trinity Foundation is not a "practical" ministry. If you are a pastor, we will not enlighten you on how to organize an ecumenical prayer meeting in your community or how to double church attendance in a year. If you are a homemaker, you will have to read elsewhere to find out how to become a total woman. If you are a businessman, we will not tell you how to develop a social conscience. The professing church is drowning in such "practical" advice.

The Trinity Foundation is unapologetically theoretical in its outlook, believing that theory without practice is dead, and that practice without theory is blind. The trouble with the professing church is not primarily in its practice, but in its theory. Christians do not know, and many do not even care to know, the doctrines of Scripture. Doctrine is intellectual, and Christians are generally anti-intellectual. Doctrine is ivory tower philosophy, and they scorn ivory towers. The ivory tower, however, is the control tower of a civilization. It is a fundamental, theoretical mistake of the practical men to think that they can be merely practical, for practice is always the practice of some theory. The relationship between theory and practice is the relationship between cause and effect. If a person believes correct theory, his practice will tend to be correct. The practice of contemporary Christians is immoral because it is the practice of false theories. It is a major theoretical mistake of the practical men to think that they can ignore the ivory towers of the philosophers and theologians as irrelevant to their lives. Every action that the "practical" men take is governed by the thinking that has occurred in some ivory tower–whether that tower be the British Museum; the Academy; a home in Basel, Switzerland; or a tent in Israel.

In Understanding Be Men

It is the first duty of the Christian to understand correct theory—correct doctrine—and thereby implement correct practice. This order—first theory, then practice—is both logical and Biblical. It is, for example, exhibited in Paul's epistle to the Romans, in which he spends the first eleven chapters expounding theory and the last five discussing practice. The contemporary teachers of Christians have not only reversed the order, they have inverted the Pauline emphasis on theory and practice. The virtually complete failure of the teachers of the professing church to instruct the faithful in correct doctrine is the cause of the misconduct and cultural impotence of Christians. The Church's lack of power is the result of its lack of truth. The *Gospel* is the power of God, not religious experience or personal relationship. The Church has no power because it has abandoned the Gospel, the good news, for a religion of experientialism. Twentieth-century American Christians are children carried about by every wind of doctrine, not knowing what they believe, or even if they believe anything for certain.

The chief purpose of The Trinity Foundation is to counteract the irrationalism of the age and to expose the errors of the teachers of the Church. Our emphasis—on the Bible as the sole source of truth, on the primacy of the intellect, on the supreme importance of correct doctrine, and on the necessity for systematic and logical thinking—is almost unique in Christendom. To the extent that the Church survives—and she will survive and flourish—it will be because of her increasing acceptance of these basic ideas and their logical implications.

We believe that the Trinity Foundation is filling a vacuum in Christendom. We are saying that Christianity is intellectually defensible—that, in fact, it is the only intellectually defensible system of thought. We are saying that God has made the wisdom of this world—whether that wisdom be called science, religion, philosophy, or common sense–foolishness. We are appealing to all Christians who have not conceded defeat in the intellectual battle with the world to join us in our efforts to raise a standard to which all men of sound mind can repair.

The love of truth, of God's Word, has all but disappeared in our time. We are committed to and pray for a great instauration. But though we may not see this reformation of Christendom in our lifetimes, we believe it is our duty to present the whole counsel of God because Christ has commanded it. The results of our teaching are in God's hands, not ours. Whatever those results, his Word is never taught in vain, but always accomplishes the result that he intended it to accomplish. Professor Gordon H. Clark has stated our view well:

> There have been times in the history of God's people, for example, in the days of Jeremiah, when refreshing grace and widespread revival were not to be expected: The time was one of chastisement. If this twentieth century is of a similar nature, individual Christians here and there can find comfort and strength in a study of God's Word. But if God has decreed happier days for us and if we may expect a world-shaking and genuine spiritual awakening, then it is the author's belief that a zeal for souls, however necessary, is not the sufficient condition. Have there not been devout saints in every age, numerous enough to carry on a revival? Twelve such persons are plenty. What distinguishes the arid ages from the period of the Reformation, when nations were moved as they had not been since Paul preached in Ephesus, Corinth, and Rome, is the latter's fullness of knowledge of God's Word. To echo an early Reformation thought, when the ploughman and the garage attendant know the Bible as well as the theologian does, and know it better than some contemporary theologians, then the desired awakening shall have already occurred.

In addition to publishing books, such as *Justification by Faith Alone*, the Foundation publishes a monthly newsletter, *The Trinity Review*. Subscriptions to *The Review* are free; please write to the address below to become a subscriber. If you would like further information or would like to join us in our work, please let us know.

The Trinity Foundation is a non-profit foundation, tax-exempt under section 501 (c)(3) of the Internal Revenue Code of 1954. You can help us disseminate the Word of God through your tax-deductible contributions to the Foundation.

And we know that the Son of God has come and has given us an understanding, that we may know him who is true; and we are in him who is true, in his Son Jesus Christ. This is the true God and eternal life.

John W. Robbins

Intellectual Ammunition

The Trinity Foundation is committed to the reformation of philosophy and theology along Biblical lines. We regard God's command to bring all our thoughts into conformity with Christ very seriously, and the books listed below are designed to accomplish that goal. They are written with two subordinate purposes: (1) to demolish all secular claims to knowledge; and (2) to build a system of truth based upon the Bible alone.

Philosophy

Behaviorism and Christianity, Gordon H. Clark $6.95
  Behaviorism *is a critique of both secular and religious behaviorists. It includes chapters on John Watson, Edgar S. Singer Jr., Gilbert Ryle, B.F. Skinner, and Donald MacKay. Clark's refutation of behaviorism and his argument for a Christian doctrine of man are unanswerable.*

A Christian Philosophy of Education $8.95
Gordon H. Clark
  The first edition of this book was published in 1946. It sparked the contemporary interest in Christian schools. Dr. Clark thoroughly revised and updated it, and it is needed now more than ever. Its chapters include: The Need for a World-View, The Christian World-View, The Alternative to Christian Theism, Neutrality, Ethics, The Christian Philosophy of Education, Academic Matters, Kindergarten to University. Three appendices are included as well: The Relationship of Public Education to Christianity, A Protestant World-View, and Art and the Gospel.

A Christian View of Men and Things $10.95
Gordon H. Clark

No other book achieves what A Christian View *does: the presentation of Christianity as it applies to history, politics, ethics, science, religion, and epistemology. Clark's command of both worldly philosophy and Scripture is evident on every page, and the result is a breathtaking and invigorating challenge to the wisdom of this world.*

Clark Speaks From The Grave, Gordon H. Clark $3.95
Dr. Clark chides some of his critics for their failure to defend Christianity competently. Clark Speaks *is a stimulating and illuminating discussion of the errors of contemporary apologists.*

Education, Christianity, and the State $9.95
J. Gresham Machen

Machen was one of the foremost educators, theologians, and defenders of Christianity in the twentieth century. The author of numerous scholarly books, Machen saw clearly that if Christianity is to survive and flourish, a system of Christian schools must be established. This collection of essays captures his thoughts on education over nearly three decades.

Essays on Ethics and Politics, Gordon H. Clark $10.95
Clark's essays, written over the course of five decades, are a major statement of Christian ethics.

Gordon H. Clark: Personal Recollections $6.95
John W. Robbins, editor

Friends of Dr. Clark have written their recollections of the man. Contributors include family members, colleagues, students, and friends such as Harold Lindsell, Carl Henry, Ronald Nash, Dwight Zeller, and Mary Crumpacker. The book includes an extensive bibliography of Clark's work.

Historiography: Secular and Religious $13.95
Gordon H. Clark
In this masterful work, Clark applies his philosophy to the writing of history, examining all the major schools of historiography.

An Introduction to Christian Philosophy $8.95
Gordon H. Clark
In 1966 Clark delivered three lectures on philosophy at Wheaton College. In these lectures he criticizes secular philosophy and launches a philosophical revolution in the name of Christ.

Language and Theology, Gordon H. Clark $9.95
There are two main currents in twentieth-century philosophy— language philosophy and existentialism. Both are hostile to Christianity. Clark disposes of language philosophy in this brilliant critique of Bertrand Russell, Ludwig Wittgenstein, Rudolf Carnap, A.J. Ayer, Langdon Gilkey, and many others.

Logic, Gordon H. Clark $8.95
Written as a textbook for Christian schools, Logic *is another unique book from Clark's pen. His presentation of the laws of thought, which must be followed if Scripture is to be understood correctly, and which are found in Scripture itself, is both clear and thorough.* Logic *is an indispensable book for the thinking Christian.*

Logic Workbook, Elihu Carranza $11.95
Designed to be used in conjunction with Clark's textbook Logic, *this* Workbook *contains hundreds of exercises and test questions on perforated pages for ease of use by students.*

Logic Workbook Answer Key, Elihu Carranza $4.95
The Key *contains answers to all the exercises and tests in the* Workbook.

Lord God of Truth, Concerning the Teacher $7.95
Gordon H. Clark and Aurelius Augustine
This essay by Clark summarizes many of the most telling arguments against empiricism and defends the Biblical teaching that we know God and truth immediately. The dialogue by Augustine is a refutation of empirical language philosophy.

The Philosophy of Science and Belief in God $5.95
Gordon H. Clark
In opposing the contemporary idolatry of science, Clark analyzes three major aspects of science: the problem of motion, Newtonian science, and modern theories of physics. His conclusion is that science, while it may be useful, is always false; and he demonstrates its falsity in numerous ways. Since science is always false, it can offer no objection to the Bible and Christianity.

Religion, Reason and Revelation, Gordon H. Clark $10.95
One of Clark's apologetical masterpieces, Religion, Reason and Revelation *has been praised for the clarity of its thought and language. It includes chapters on Is Christianity a Religion? Faith and Reason, Inspiration and Language, Revelation and Morality, and God and Evil. It is must reading for all serious Christians.*

Thales to Dewey: A History of Philosophy   paper $11.95
Gordon H. Clark   hardback $16.95
This is the best one-volume history of philosophy in English.

Three Types of Religious Philosophy, Gordon H. Clark $6.95
In this book on apologetics, Clark examines empiricism, rationalism, dogmatism, and contemporary irrationalism, which does not rise to the level of philosophy. He offers a solution to the question, "How can Christianity be defended before the world?"

William James and John Dewey $8.95
Gordon H. Clark
William James and John Dewey are two of the most influential phi-
losophers America has produced. Their philosophies of instru-
mentalism and pragmatism are hostile to Christianity, and Clark de-
molishes their arguments.

Theology

The Atonement, Gordon H. Clark $8.95
In The Atonement, *Clark discusses the covenants, the virgin birth*
and incarnation, federal headship and representation, the relationship
between God's sovereignty and justice, and much more. He analyzes
traditional views of the atonement and criticizes them in the light of
Scripture alone.

The Biblical Doctrine of Man, Gordon H. Clark $6.95
Is man soul and body or soul, spirit, and body? What is the image
of God? Is Adam's sin imputed to his children? Is evolution true? Are
men totally depraved? What is the heart? These are some of the ques-
tions discussed and answered from Scripture in this book.

The Clark–Van Til Controversy, Herman Hoeksema $5.95
This collection of essays by the founder of the Protestant Reformed
Church–essays written at the time of the Clark–Van Til controversy–
is one of the best commentaries on the events yet written.

Cornelius Van Til: The Man and The Myth $2.45
John W. Robbins
The actual teachings of this eminent Philadelphia theologian have
been obscured by the myths that surround him. This book penetrates
those myths and criticizes Van Til's surprisingly unorthodox views of
God and the Bible.

The Everlasting Righteousness, Horatius Bonar $8.95
Originally published in 1874, the language of Bonar's masterpiece on justification by faith alone has been updated and Americanized for easy reading and clear understanding. This is one of the best books ever written on justification.

Faith and Saving Faith, Gordon H. Clark $6.95
The views of the Roman Catholic church, John Calvin, Thomas Manton, John Owen, Charles Hodge, and B.B. Warfield are discussed in this book. Is the object of faith a person or a proposition? Is faith more than belief? Is belief more than thinking with assent, as Augustine said? In a world chaotic with differing views of faith, Clark clearly explains the Biblical view of faith and saving faith.

God's Hammer: The Bible and Its Critics $10.95
Gordon H. Clark
The starting point of Christianity, the doctrine on which all other doctrines depend, is "The Bible alone is the Word of God written, and therefore inerrant in the autographs." Over the centuries the opponents of Christianity, with Satanic shrewdness, have concentrated their attacks on the truthfulness and completeness of the Bible. In the twentieth century the attack is not so much in the fields of history and archaeology as in philosophy. Clark's brilliant defense of the complete truthfulness of the Bible is captured in this collection of eleven major essays.

Guide to the Westminster Confession and Catechism $13.95
James E. Bordwine
This large book contains the full text of both the Westminster Confession (both original and American versions) and the Larger Catechism. In addition, it offers a chapter-by-chapter summary of the Confession and a unique index to both the Confession and the Catechism.

The Holy Spirit, Gordon H. Clark $8.95
   This discussion of the third person of the Trinity is both concise and exact. Clark includes chapters on the work of the Spirit, santification, and Pentecostalism. This book is part of his multi-volume systematic theology that began appearing in print in 1985.

The Incarnation, Gordon H. Clark $8.95
   Who is Christ? The attack on the incarnation in the nineteenth and twentieth centuries has been vigorous, but the orthodox response has been lame. Clark reconstructs the doctrine of the incarnation, building and improving upon the Chalcedonian definition.

In Defense of Theology, Gordon H. Clark $9.95
   There are four groups to whom Clark addresses this book: average Christians who are uninterested in theology, atheists and agnostics, religious experientialists, and serious Christians. The vindication of the knowledge of God against the objections of three of these groups is the first step in theology.

The Johannine Logos, Gordon H. Clark $5.95
   Clark analyzes the relationship between Christ, who is the truth, and the Bible. He explains why John used the same word to refer to both Christ and his teaching. Chapters deal with the Prologue to John's Gospel, Logos and Rheemata, Truth, and Saving Faith.

Justification by Faith Alone, Charles Hodge $10.95
   Charles Hodge of Princeton Seminary was the best American theologian of the nineteenth century. Here in one volume are his two major essays on justification. This book is essential in defending the faith.

Predestination, Gordon H. Clark $8.95
   Clark thoroughly discusses one of the most controversial and pervasive doctrines of the Bible: that God is, quite literally, Almighty. Free will, the origin of evil, God's omniscience, creation, and the

new birth are all presented within a Scriptural framework. The objections of those who do not believe in the Almighty God are considered and refuted. This edition also contains the text of the booklet, Predestination in the Old Testament.

Sanctification, Gordon H. Clark $8.95
    In this book, which is part of Clark's multi-volume systematic theology, he discusses historical theories of sanctification, the sacraments, and the Biblical doctrine of sanctification.

Today's Evangelism: Counterfeit or Genuine? $6.95
Gordon H. Clark
    Clark compares the methods and messages of today's evangelists with Scripture, and finds that Christianity is on the wane because the Gospel has been distorted or lost. This is an extremely useful and enlightening book.

The Trinity, Gordon H. Clark $8.95
    Apart from the doctrine of Scripture, no teaching of the Bible is more important than the doctrine of God. Clark's defense of the orthodox doctrine of the Trinity is a principal portion of Clark's systematic theology. There are chapters on the deity of Christ, Augustine, the incomprehensibility of God, Bavinck and Van Til, and the Holy Spirit, among others.

What Calvin Says, W. Gary Crampton $7.95
    This is both a readable and thorough introduction to the theology of John Calvin.

What Do Presbyterians Believe? Gordon H. Clark $8.95
    This classic introduction to Christian doctrine has been republished. It is the best commentary on the Westminster Confession of Faith that has ever been written.

Commentaries on the New Testament

Colossians, Gordon H. Clark	$ 6.95
Ephesians, Gordon H. Clark	$ 8.95
First Corinthians, Gordon H. Clark	$10.95
First John, Gordon H. Clark	$10.95
First and Second Thessalonians, Gordon H. Clark	$ 5.95
New Heavens, New Earth (First and Second Peter) Gordon H. Clark	$10.95
The Pastoral Epistles (I and II Timothy and Titus) Gordon H. Clark	$ 9.95

All of Clark's commentaries are expository, not technical, and are written for the Christian layman. His purpose is to explain the text clearly and accurately so that the Word of God will be thoroughly known by every Christian.

The Trinity Library

We will send you one copy of each of the 45 books listed above for $250. You may also order the books you want individually on the order blank on the next page. Because some of the books are in short supply, we must reserve the right to substitute others of equal or greater value in The Trinity Library. This special offer expires June 30, 1997.

ORDER FORM

Name _____

Address _____

_____

Please: ☐ add my name to the mailing list for *The Trinity Review*.
I understand that there is no charge for the *Review* in
the United States. (Ten dollars per year to foreign addresses.)

☐ accept my tax deductible contribution of $ _____
for the work of the Foundation.

☐ send me _____ copies of *Justification by Faith
Alone*. I enclose as payment $_____

☐ send me the Trinity Library of 45 books.
I enclose $250 as full payment.

☐ send me the following books. I enclose full payment in
the amount of $ _____ for them.

_____

_____

_____

_____

_____

_____

Mail to:

The Trinity Foundation
Post Office Box 1666
Hobbs, New Mexico 88240